GW00691433

COOK'S COLLECTION

# CAKES & BAKES

Fuss-free and tasty recipe ideas for the modern cook

CONTENTS

# INTRODUCTION

Home baking is one of life's great pleasures. If you ask anyone who enjoys cooking which recipes they love to make the most, it's bound to be a cake or a dessert! Probably because something as simple as a freshly baked sponge, a batch of spicy biscuits or a fragrant fruit pie gives the cook such immense satisfaction, and the enjoyment of those who sample the results is always very rewarding.

With everyone's lives led at a fast pace, quite often baking from scratch will get put to one side. There's such a huge selection of baked treats to tempt you at the supermarket and bakery, it's easy to just take the simple option and add them to your basket. But nothing tastes as good as the real thing and you'll know exactly what's gone into the recipe too. There'll be no preservatives or additives, artificial colourings or flavourings – just good wholesome ingredients.

A quick glance at the many recipes included in *Cakes & Bakes* will make your mouth water and surely spur you on to get out the scales, check your store cupboard for stocks of flour and sugar and whip up a batch of goodies. If baking is something you've wanted to try and not quite had the courage to attempt, look no further! There are over 100 easy-to-follow recipes in this book for cakes and cookies, pies and pastries and bread, both sweet and savoury. And if you're baking for people with dietary concerns or just fancy a change, Gluten-Free, Low-Sugar and Vegan recipes are also included and none of the ingredients are hard to find. The recipes are easy to follow and won't take up too much of your time either.

Why not try luscious Lemon Drizzle Cake (see page 16) or make a batch of Chocolate Chip Cookies (see page 86) to take to work. How about Cheese, Chilli & Potato Empanadas (see page 182) for a great addition to anyone's lunch box? And who can resist the smell of freshly baked bread? There are some really great recipes to try, such as tasty Sourdough Bread (see page 158), healthy Wholemeal Carrot Rolls (see page 172) or Chocolate & Saffron Brioche (see page 178).

If you've never tried baking with yeast, now's the time to experiment. There are plenty of old favourites to choose from as well as some new ideas to try, so what are you waiting for?

Before you get going, it's a good idea to have some basic utensils and equipment. As you become more experienced and adventurous, you'll probably want to invest in the more specialized items available in the shops. On-line companies have huge selections too, which will save time searching for just the right size of tin or special ingredient. But to get started, a set of scales is essential for weighing ingredients correctly. A selection of bowls in different sizes, measuring and wooden spoons, and a plastic spatula for scraping out mixtures are all important. A hand-held electric mixer will make light work of mixing.

Using the wrong sized baking tin in can produce disappointing results, so have a range of different sizes to hand. You'll need baking paper to prevent cakes getting stuck – even if your tins are non-stick it's better to be safe than sorry! You can buy ready-cut liners to save time and wire racks for cooling are useful too. It's a good idea to check the sell-by dates on flour, yeast, baking powder and baking soda. They're the ingredients that help give the all-important rise to most recipes and should be replaced if stale. Always use fresh eggs as this improves the flavour. Dried spices and herbs loose their pungency if they've been in the cupboard for too long.

Have all your ingredients weighed out, sifted, softened – whatever the recipe states – before you start. This saves time and also ensures that no ingredients are missed out. Place your oven racks in the right position before you turn on the oven, and if you think the temperature is a little unreliable, an oven thermometer is a great tool. If you need to divide the mixture between more than one tin, use your scales to make sure you have even amounts in each. This will ensure an even bake.

Once your tins or trays are in the oven, don't be tempted to open the door too soon as this can cause some recipes to collapse. Insert a cake tester or wooden skewer into the centre of your cakes and buns to check there is no uncooked mixture before taking them out. Don't turn them out of their tins too soon – allow them to cool enough to shrink from the sides, then use a round-ended knife to run round the outside edge of the cake before tipping it onto a wire rack. Similarly, when making cookies or small cakes, allow them to set before removing them from the tins. When baking bread, tap the base of the loaf with your knuckles. If it sounds hollow it's done.

Home-baked treats keep well too. Biscuits will stay crisp in an airtight container for several days and fruit cakes really improve if left to mature before cutting. Most cakes freeze well, although they are best iced after thawing – freezing is a great way to get ahead if you're expecting visitors or have a celebration coming up.

When you get the time, have a day in the kitchen. It will give you the chance to try out new skills and delicious recipes, have plenty of goodies to offer friends, take to work or just enjoy at home when you fancy. The family will love tasting the fruits of your labour but you needn't be the only baker in the house. Kids love getting involved, especially if they can personalize the results. Icing cupcakes, dipping biscotti or just creating their own shaped bread rolls is great fun, and they get to eat them too! So roll up your sleeves and get your apron on – prepare to become the most popular cook around!

CHAPTER ONE

# CAKES

# CELEBRATION CHOCOLATE CAKE

**SERVES:** *8* | **PREP:** *40 mins* | **COOK:** *1 hour 20 mins, plus cooling*

**INGREDIENTS**

*2 raw beetroot, cut into cubes, about 200 g/7 oz*
*150 g/5½ oz plain chocolate with 70% cocoa solids, broken into pieces*
*25 g/1 oz cocoa powder*
*2 tsp baking powder*
*115 g/4 oz wholemeal plain flour*
*55 g/2 oz brown rice flour*
*200 g/7 oz unsalted butter, softened and diced, plus extra for greasing*
*215 g/7½ oz light muscovado sugar*
*4 eggs*
*2 tbsp milk*
*300 ml/10 fl oz double cream*

*1.* Preheat the oven to 160°C/325°F/Gas Mark 3. Lightly grease a 20-cm/8-inch round non-stick springform cake tin and line the base with baking paper. Place the beetroot in a steamer and steam for 15 minutes, or until tender. Transfer to a food processor and add 4 tablespoons of water from the base of the steamer. Purée until smooth, then leave to cool.

*2.* Put 115 g/4 oz of the chocolate in a heatproof bowl set over a saucepan of gently simmering water, and heat until melted. Sift the cocoa into a separate bowl, then stir in the baking powder, wholemeal flour and rice flour. Cream the butter and 200 g/7 oz of the sugar in a large bowl.

*3.* Beat in the eggs, one at a time, alternating with spoonfuls of the flour mixture, and beating well after each addition. Stir in the remaining flour mixture, the puréed beetroot and melted chocolate and beat until smooth, then mix in enough of the milk to make a soft dropping consistency.

*4.* Spoon the mixture into the prepared tin and spread it in an even layer. Bake in the preheated oven for 1 hour, or until well risen. Leave to cool in the tin for 15 minutes, then turn out, peel off the baking paper, transfer the cake to a wire rack and leave to cool completely.

*5.* Put the remaining chocolate in a heatproof bowl set over a saucepan of gently simmering water and heat until melted. Put the cream in a bowl, add the remaining sugar and whip until it holds soft peaks. Cut the cake in half and put the bottom half on a serving plate. Spoon one third of the cream mixture onto the base of the cake, add the top half of the cake, then spoon the remaining cream on the top. Drizzle with the melted chocolate. Cut into eight wedges to serve.

# PISTACHIO & ROSE LAYER CAKE

**SERVES:** *10* | **PREP:** *45 mins* | **COOK:** *20 mins, plus cooling*

**INGREDIENTS**

*225 g/8 oz soft light brown sugar*
*225 g/8 oz unsalted butter, softened, plus extra for greasing*
*4 eggs*
*165 g/5¾ oz self-raising flour*
*65 g/2¼ oz ground almonds*
*½ tsp ground cinnamon*
*seeds from 6 green cardamom pods, crushed*

**ROSE MASCARPONE FROSTING**

*750 g/1 lb 10 oz mascarpone cheese*
*150 g/5½ oz icing sugar*
*¼ tsp rosewater*
*3 drops pink food colouring (optional)*
*40 g/1½ oz pistachio nuts, roughly chopped*
*1 tbsp dried rose petals or fresh edible rose petals, to decorate (optional)*

*1.* Preheat the oven to 180°C/350°F/Gas Mark 4. Grease three 20-cm/8-inch round springform cake tins and line with baking paper.

*2.* Using a hand-held electric mixer or wooden spoon, beat the brown sugar and butter together in a large bowl until well mixed. Beat in the eggs, one at a time, whisking well after each addition. Sprinkle a little of the flour in with each egg to prevent the mixture splitting.

*3.* In a separate bowl, mix the flour, almonds and cinnamon together, then stir the crushed cardamom seeds into the flour mixture.

*4.* Fold the flour mixture into the eggs until incorporated. Divide between the prepared tins, level the tops and bake in the preheated oven for 20 minutes, until a skewer inserted into the centre of the cakes comes out clean. Leave the cakes to cool in the tins for 10 minutes, then transfer to a wire rack and leave to cool completely.

*5.* To make the frosting, put the mascarpone cheese into a large bowl and beat with a hand-held electric mixer or wooden spoon until smooth. Whisk in the icing sugar, rosewater and enough food colouring, if using, to give a very pale pink colour. Spoon the frosting into a piping bag fitted with a plain nozzle.

*6.* Pipe one third of the frosting over one of the cakes in small minaret-shaped rounds, then sprinkle with pistachio nuts. Add another cake and pipe over half the remaining frosting in rounds, followed by more pistachio nuts. Add the final cake, then pipe rounds over it in a design of your choice, before sprinkling with the remaining pistachio nuts and the rose petals, if using.

# VICTORIA SPONGE CAKE

**SERVES:** *8* | **PREP:** *30 mins* | **COOK:** *25–30 mins*

**INGREDIENTS**

*175 g/6 oz self-raising flour*
*1 tsp baking powder*
*175 g/6 oz butter, softened, plus extra for greasing*
*175 g/6 oz golden caster sugar*
*3 eggs*
*icing sugar, for dusting*

**FILLING**

*3 tbsp raspberry jam*
*300 ml/10 fl oz double cream, whipped*
*16 fresh strawberries, halved*

*1.* Preheat the oven to 180°C/350°F/Gas Mark 4. Grease two 20-cm/8-inch sandwich tins and line with baking paper.

*2.* Sift the flour and baking powder into a bowl and add the butter, sugar and eggs. Mix together, then beat well until smooth.

*3.* Divide the mixture between the prepared tins and smooth the surfaces. Bake in the preheated oven for 25–30 minutes, or until the cakes are well risen, golden brown and springy to the touch.

*4.* Leave to cool in the tins for 5 minutes, then turn out and peel off the baking paper. Transfer the cakes to wire racks and leave to cool completely. Sandwich the cakes together with the jam, cream and strawberry halves. Dust with icing sugar and serve.

# CHOCOLATE FUDGE CAKE

**SERVES:** *8* | **PREP:** *35 mins, plus cooling & chilling* | **COOK:** *35–40 mins*

**INGREDIENTS**

*175 g/6 oz butter, softened, plus extra for greasing*
*175 g/6 oz golden caster sugar*
*3 eggs, beaten*
*3 tbsp golden syrup*
*40 g/1½ oz ground almonds*
*175 g/6 oz self-raising flour*
*pinch of salt*
*40 g/1½ oz cocoa powder*

**FROSTING**

*225 g/8 oz plain chocolate, broken into pieces*
*55 g/2 oz muscovado sugar*
*225 g/8 oz butter, diced*
*5 tbsp evaporated milk*
*½ tsp vanilla extract*

*1.* Preheat the oven to 180°C/350°F/Gas Mark 4. Grease two 20-cm/8-inch sandwich tins and line with baking paper.

*2.* To make the frosting, place the chocolate, muscovado sugar, butter, evaporated milk and vanilla extract in a saucepan. Heat gently, stirring constantly, until the chocolate has melted. Pour into a bowl and leave to cool. Cover and chill in the refrigerator for 1 hour, or until spreadable.

*3.* Place the butter and caster sugar in a large bowl and beat together until light and creamy. Gradually beat in the eggs. Stir in the golden syrup and ground almonds. Sift the flour, salt and cocoa powder into a separate bowl, then fold into the mixture. Add a little water, if necessary, to make a dropping consistency.

*4.* Divide the mixture evenly between the prepared tins and smooth the surfaces. Bake in the preheated oven for 30–35 minutes, or until risen and springy to the touch.

*5.* Leave in the tins to cool slightly, then turn out, transfer to a wire rack and leave to cool completely. Sandwich the cooled cakes together with half the frosting. Spread the remaining frosting over the top and sides of the cake, swirling it to give a frosted appearance.

# GLUTEN- & DAIRY-FREE ORANGE & ALMOND CAKE

**SERVES:** *8* | **PREP:** *30 mins* | **COOK:** *2 hours 35 mins–3 hours 5 mins*

**INGREDIENTS**

*375 g/13 oz oranges (about 2 small oranges)*
*olive oil, for oiling*
*6 eggs*
*225 g/8 oz muscovado sugar*
*250 g/9 oz ground almonds*
*1 tsp gluten-free baking powder*
*½ tsp ground cloves*

**FIG TOPPING**

*4 plump figs, cut into segments*
*25 g/1 oz sliced almonds, toasted*
*zest of 1 orange*

*1.* Place the oranges in a large saucepan with some cold water. Bring to a gentle simmer and cook for 1½–2 hours. Drain and leave to cool. Cut each orange in half and remove the pips. Put the oranges – skins, pith and fruit – into a blender or food processor and blitz.

*2.* Preheat the oven to 190°C/375°F/Gas Mark 5. Grease a 20-cm/8-inch round springform cake tin and line with baking paper.

*3.* Place the eggs in a mixing bowl and gently whisk. Add the sugar, almonds, baking powder and cloves and mix well, then stir through the pulped oranges.

*4.* Pour the mixture into the prepared tin and bake in the preheated oven for 1 hour, or until golden and a skewer inserted in the centre comes out clean. Remove from the oven, place the tin on a wire rack and leave to cool completely. Remove from the tin.

*5.* Decorate the cake with the figs, toasted almonds and orange zest.

# LEMON DRIZZLE CAKE

**SERVES:** *8* | **PREP:** *20 mins* | **COOK:** *45 mins–1 hour*

**INGREDIENTS**

*butter, for greasing*
*200 g/7 oz plain flour*
*2 tsp baking powder*
*200 g/7 oz caster sugar*
*4 eggs*
*150 ml/5 fl oz soured cream*
*grated rind of 1 large lemon*
*4 tbsp lemon juice*
*150 ml/5 fl oz sunflower oil*

**SYRUP**

*4 tbsp icing sugar*
*3 tbsp lemon juice*

*1.* Preheat the oven to 180°C/350°F/Gas Mark 4. Grease a 20-cm/8-inch round cake tin and line with baking paper.

*2.* Sift the flour and baking powder into a large bowl and stir in the caster sugar.

*3.* In a separate bowl, whisk together the eggs, soured cream, lemon rind, lemon juice and oil.

*4.* Pour the egg mixture into the dry ingredients and mix well until evenly combined.

*5.* Spoon the mixture into the prepared tin and bake in the preheated oven for 45 minutes–1 hour, or until risen, golden and springy to the touch.

*6.* Meanwhile, to make the syrup, mix the icing sugar and lemon juic together in a small saucepan. Stir over a low heat until just beginnin to bubble and turn syrupy.

*7.* As soon as the cake comes out of the oven, prick the surface with a fine skewer, then brush the syrup over the top. Leave the cake to coo completely in the tin, then turn out and serve.

2
3
4

# SPINACH & APPLE CAKE WITH APPLE ICING

**SERVES:** *12* | **PREP:** *15–20 mins* | **COOK:** *30–35 mins, plus cooling*

**INGREDIENTS**

*500 g/1 lb 2 oz baby spinach*
*250 g/9 oz spelt flour*
*1 tbsp baking powder*
*½ tsp salt*
*3 eggs*
*150 g/5½ oz golden caster sugar*
*125 ml/4 fl oz rapeseed oil, plus extra for oiling*
*3 tbsp lemon juice*
*100 g/3½ oz eating apple, roughly grated*
*2 tsp vanilla extract*

**ICING**

*2 cooking apples, cut into large chunks*
*225 g/8 oz icing sugar, sifted*
*25 g/1 oz butter, softened*
*½ tsp finely grated lemon peel*

*1.* Preheat the oven to 180°C/350°F/Gas Mark 4. Oil a 22-cm/8½-inch square cake tin and line with baking paper.

*2.* Put the spinach into a steamer and steam for 3 minutes, then squeeze dry, transfer to a blender and purée until smooth. Set aside until needed.

*3.* Sift together the flour, baking powder and salt twice into a bowl. Put the eggs and sugar into a separate large bowl and beat with a hand-held electric mixer for 5 minutes, or until pale and creamy. Lightly whisk in the oil, lemon juice, apple, vanilla extract and spinach purée. Gradually stir in the flour mixture.

*4.* Pour the mixture into the prepared tin. Bake in the preheated oven for 25–30 minutes, or until a skewer inserted into the centre comes out clean. Leave to cool in the tin for 10 minutes, then turn out onto a wire rack and leave to cool completely.

*5.* Using a sharp serrated knife, trim about 1½ cm/⅝ inch from all four sides of the cake. Scoop out the green part from underneath these crusts, rub into crumbs using your fingertips and set aside.

*6.* To make the icing, put the apples into a saucepan with a little water, bring to a simmer over a medium–low heat and cook until soft. Mash with a fork, then push through a sieve into a bowl. Add the remaining ingredients and mix well together. Spoon over the top of the cake and sprinkle with a few of the reserved green crumbs. Slice into squares to serve.

2

3

4

# RED VELVET CAKE

**SERVES:** *12* | **PREP:** *30 mins, plus cooling* | **COOK:** *35–40 mins*

**INGREDIENTS**

*225 g/8 oz unsalted butter, plus extra for greasing*
*4 tbsp water*
*55 g/2 oz cocoa powder*
*3 eggs*
*250 ml/9 fl oz buttermilk*
*2 tsp vanilla extract*
*2 tbsp red food colouring*
*280 g/10 oz plain flour*
*55 g/2 oz cornflour*
*1½ tsp baking powder*
*280 g/10 oz caster sugar*

**FROSTING**

*250 g/9 oz cream cheese*
*40 g/1½ oz unsalted butter*
*3 tbsp caster sugar*
*1 tsp vanilla extract*

*1.* Preheat the oven to 190°C/375°F/Gas Mark 5. Grease two 23-cm/9-inch sandwich tins and line with baking paper.

*2.* Place the butter, water and cocoa powder in a small saucepan and gently heat, without boiling, stirring constantly, until melted and smooth. Remove from the heat and leave to cool slightly.

*3.* Beat together the eggs, buttermilk, vanilla extract and food colouring until frothy. Beat in the butter mixture. Sift in the flour, cornflour and baking powder, then stir quickly and evenly into the mixture with the sugar.

*4.* Spoon the mixture into the prepared tins and bake in the preheated oven for 25–30 minutes, or until risen and firm to the touch. Leave to cool in the tins for 3–4 minutes, then turn out onto a wire rack and leave to cool completely.

*5.* To make the frosting, beat together all the ingredients until smooth. Use about half of the frosting to sandwich the cakes together, then spread the remainder over the top, swirling with a palette knife.

# CLASSIC FRUIT CAKE

**SERVES:** *16* | **PREP:** *35 mins, plus soaking, cooling & storing* | **COOK:** *2¼–2¾ hours*

**INGREDIENTS**

*350 g/12 oz sultanas*
*225 g/8 oz raisins*
*115 g/4 oz ready-to-eat dried apricots, chopped*
*85 g/3 oz dried ready-to-eat dates, stoned and chopped*
*4 tbsp dark rum or brandy, plus extra for flavouring (optional)*
*finely grated rind and juice of 1 orange*
*225 g/8 oz butter, softened, plus extra for greasing*
*225 g/8 oz light muscovado sugar*
*4 eggs, beaten*
*70 g/2½ oz chopped mixed peel*
*85 g/3 oz glacé cherries, quartered*
*25 g/1 oz chopped glacé ginger or stem ginger*
*40 g/1½ oz blanched almonds, chopped*
*200 g/7 oz plain flour*
*1 tsp mixed spice*

*1.* Place the sultanas, raisins, apricots and dates in a large bowl and stir in the rum, orange rind and orange juice. Cover and leave to soak for several hours or overnight.

*2.* Preheat the oven to 150°C/300°F/Gas Mark 2. Grease a 20-cm/8-inch deep round cake tin and line with baking paper.

*3.* Put the butter and sugar in a large bowl and beat together until light and creamy. Gradually add the eggs, beating after each addition. Stir in the soaked fruits, mixed peel, glacé cherries, glacé ginger and blanched almonds.

*4.* Sift in the flour and mixed spice, then fold lightly and evenly into the mixture. Spoon the mixture into the prepared tin, making a depression in the centre with the back of the spoon.

*5.* Bake in the preheated oven for 2¼–2¾ hours, or until risen and springy to the touch. Leave to cool in the tin for 5 minutes, then turn out of the tin, transfer to a wire rack and leave to cool completely.

*6.* Wrap the cooled cake in greaseproof paper and foil. Store for at least 2 months before eating. To add a richer flavour, prick the cake with a skewer and spoon over a couple of extra tablespoons of rum or brandy, if using, before wrapping and storing.

1

3

4

# GINGER OAT CAKE

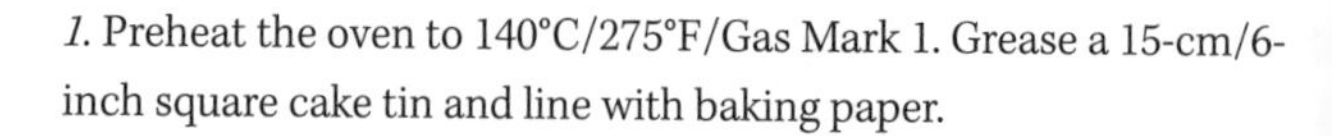

**SERVES:** *10–12* | **PREP:** *20 mins, plus cooling & storing* | **COOK:** *1 hour 50 mins–2 hours 5 mins*

**INGREDIENTS**

*150 g/5½ oz self-raising flour*
*pinch of salt*
*½ tsp mixed spice*
*2 tsp ground ginger*
*200 g/7 oz oatmeal*
*175 g/6 oz black treacle*
*100 g/3½ oz butter, plus extra for greasing*
*85 g/3 oz soft light brown sugar*
*1 tbsp milk*
*1 egg, beaten*

*1.* Preheat the oven to 140°C/275°F/Gas Mark 1. Grease a 15-cm/6-inch square cake tin and line with baking paper.

*2.* Sift the flour into a large bowl and stir in the salt, mixed spice, ginger and oatmeal. Make a well in the centre.

*3.* Place the treacle, butter and sugar in a saucepan and heat slowly over a low heat, without allowing the mixture to boil, until the butter is melted. Pour the mixture into the well in the dry ingredients and gently combine. Stir in the milk and egg and mix until smooth.

*4.* Spoon the mixture into the prepared tin and bake in the preheated oven for 1¾–2 hours, or until risen and springy to the touch.

*5.* Leave to cool in the tin for 5 minutes, then transfer to a wire rack and leave to cool completely. Store in an airtight container in a cool place for at least a week before cutting and serving, to allow it to become moist and sticky.

# BANANA BREAD LOAF

**SERVES:** *6* | **PREP:** *20 mins, plus cooling* | **COOK:** *45 mins*

**INGREDIENTS**

*225 g/8 oz vegetable fat, plus extra for greasing*
*90 g/3¼ oz sugar*
*150 g/5½ oz plain flour*
*3 tsp baking powder*
*1 tsp bicarbonate of soda*
*1 tsp salt*
*2 tbsp water*
*2 eggs, beaten*
*3 ripe bananas, mashed*

*1.* Preheat the oven to 160°C/325°F/Gas Mark 3. Grease a 450-g/1-lb loaf tin and line with baking paper.

*2.* Place the vegetable fat and sugar in a large bowl and beat together until light and creamy. Sift in the flour, baking powder, bicarbonate of soda and salt and fold in gently. Add the water and eggs and mix together to combine.

*3.* Add the mashed bananas and stir to combine. Spoon the mixture into the prepared tin. Use a spatula dipped in a little oil to score an impression along the centre of the loaf.

*4.* Bake in the preheated oven for 45 minutes, or until risen, golden and springy to the touch. Leave to cool in the tin for 5 minutes, then transfer to a wire rack to cool completely.

# VEGAN CARROT CAKE

**SERVES:** *8* | **PREP:** *20 mins, plus cooling & chilling* | **COOK:** *40–45 mins*

**INGREDIENTS**

*1 tbsp vegetable oil, for oiling*
*150 g/5½ oz dried dates*
*150 g/5½ oz sultanas*
*250 ml/9 fl oz boiling water*
*100 g/3½ oz walnuts*
*100 g/3½ oz carrots, grated*
*300 g/10½ oz plain wholemeal flour*
*1 tsp ground cinnamon*
*1 tsp baking powder*
*1 tsp bicarbonate of soda*
*125 ml/4 fl oz apple juice*

**ICING**

*100 g/3½ oz cashew nuts*
*3 tbsp maple syrup*
*1 tsp vanilla extract*
*1 tsp ground cinnamon*
*zest of 1 lemon*

*1.* Preheat the oven to 180°C/350°F/Gas Mark 4. Oil an 18-cm/7-inch round loose-based cake tin and line with baking paper.

*2.* Stone and roughly chop the dates. Place them in a small bowl with the sultanas, add the boiling water and set aside to soak.

*3.* Meanwhile, roughly chop the walnuts and place in a large mixing bowl with the carrots. Add the flour, cinnamon, baking powder and bicarbonate of soda and mix thoroughly.

*4.* Add the dates and sultanas with the soaking water and the apple juice and mix thoroughly. Spoon into the prepared tin and smooth the top with a rubber spatula.

*5.* Bake in the centre of the preheated oven for 40–45 minutes until cooked through and a skewer inserted into the centre of the cake comes out clean. Leave to cool in the tin for 10 minutes, then turn out onto a wire rack and leave to cool completely.

*6.* To make the icing, soak the nuts in boiling water for 30 minutes, then drain. Put the nuts, maple syrup, vanilla extract and cinnamon into a blender and process until smooth. Stir in the lemon zest and chill in the refrigerator for 20 minutes before spreading evenly over the top of the cake.

# ORANGE & POPPY SEED BUNDT CAKE

**SERVES:** *10* | **PREP:** *10 mins* | **COOK:** *35 mins*

**INGREDIENTS**

*200 g/7 oz unsalted butter, plus extra for greasing*
*200 g/7 oz golden caster sugar*
*3 large eggs, beaten*
*finely grated rind of 1 orange*
*55 g/2 oz poppy seeds*
*300 g/10½ oz plain flour, plus extra for dusting*
*2 tsp baking powder*
*150 ml/5 fl oz milk*
*125 ml/4 fl oz orange juice*
*strips of orange zest, to decorate*

**SYRUP**

*140 g/5 oz golden caster sugar*
*150 ml/5 fl oz orange juice*

*1.* Preheat the oven to 160°C/325°F/Gas Mark 3. Grease a 24-cm/9½ inch bundt tin and lightly dust with flour.

*2.* Cream together the butter and sugar until pale and fluffy, then gradually add the eggs, beating well after each addition. Stir in the orange rind and poppy seeds. Sift in the flour and baking powder, then fold in. Add the milk and orange juice, stirring to mix evenly.

*3.* Spoon the mixture into the prepared tin and bake in the preheated oven for 45–50 minutes, or until firm and golden brown. Leave to cool in the tin for 10 minutes, then turn out onto a wire rack.

*4.* To make the syrup, place the sugar and orange juice in a saucepan and heat over a low heat until the sugar is melted. Bring to the boil and simmer for about 5 minutes until reduced and syrupy.

*5.* Spoon the syrup over the cake while it is still warm. Top with the strips of orange zest and serve warm or cold.

# CHOCOLATE MARBLE CAKE

**SERVES:** *8* | **PREP:** *35–40 mins, plus cooling* | **COOK:** *45 mins*

**INGREDIENTS**

*sunflower oil, for oiling*
*100 g/3½ oz plain flour, plus extra for dusting*
*3 tbsp cocoa powder*
*225 g/8 oz caster sugar*
*pinch of salt*
*10 egg whites*
*1 tsp cream of tartar*
*½ tsp almond extract*
*½ tsp vanilla extract*
*icing sugar, for dusting*

*1.* Preheat the oven to 180°C/350°F/Gas Mark 4. Oil a 20-cm/8-inch round cake tin and dust with flour.

*2.* Sift 40 g/1½ oz of the flour with the cocoa powder and 2 tablespoons of the caster sugar into a bowl. Sift this mixture a further three times. Sift the remaining flour with 2 tablespoons of the sugar and the salt into a separate bowl. Sift this mixture a further three times.

*3.* Whisk the egg whites in a clean, grease-free bowl until they hold soft peaks. Add the cream of tartar and beat in the remaining caster sugar, 1 tablespoon at a time, until they hold stiff peaks. Whisk in the almond and vanilla extract. Divide the mixture in half. Fold the cocoa and flour mixture into one half and fold the unflavoured flour into the other half. Spoon the cocoa-flavoured mixture into the prepared tin and top with the unflavoured mixture. Run a round-bladed knife through both mixtures to create a marbled effect.

*4.* Bake in the preheated oven for 45 minutes, or until risen and springy to the touch. Leave to cool in the tin slightly, then transfer to a wire rack and leave to cool completely. Dust with icing sugar just before serving.

# PINEAPPLE UPSIDE-DOWN CAKE

**SERVES:** *6* | **PREP:** *30–35 mins, plus cooling* | **COOK:** *50–55 mins*

**INGREDIENTS**

*115 g/4 oz butter*
*225 g/8 oz soft light brown sugar*
*550 g/1 lb 4 oz canned pineapple rings, plus 4 tbsp juice from the can*
*7 maraschino cherries*
*12 pecan nut halves*
*3 egg yolks*
*200 g/7 oz caster sugar*
*115 g/4 oz plain flour*
*1 tsp baking powder*
*½ tsp salt*
*1 tsp vanilla extract*
*2 egg whites*

*1.* Preheat the oven to 180°C/350°F/Gas Mark 4. Melt the butter in an 25-cm/10-inch flameproof casserole dish over a low heat. Scatter the brown sugar into the dish and remove it from the heat.

*2.* Arrange 7 pineapple rings over the sugar mixture in the dish. Cut the remaining pineapple rings in half horizontally and use to line the sides of the dish. Place a cherry in the centre of each ring, then divide the pecan halves between the rings.

*3.* Beat the egg yolks with a hand-held electric mixer until thick and lemony in colour. Gradually add the caster sugar, beating well. Sift the flour, baking powder and salt into a separate bowl and stir. Add the dry ingredients to the egg mixture, alternating with the pineapple juice, mixing well. Stir in the vanilla extract.

*4.* Whisk the egg whites in a clean, grease-free bowl until they hold stiff peaks. Fold into the batter. Spoon the batter evenly over the pineapples and bake in the preheated oven for 45–50 minutes, or until the cake is set. Leave to cool slightly before turning out onto a serving plate.

2
2
3

# PECAN COFFEE LAYER CAKE

**SERVES:** *10–12* | **PREP:** *30 mins* | **COOK:** *20–25 mins*

**INGREDIENTS**

*280 g/10 oz self-raising flour*
*1 tsp baking powder*
*280 g/10 oz butter, softened, plus extra for greasing*
*280 g/10 oz caster sugar*
*5 eggs, beaten*
*1 tbsp instant coffee granules, dissolved in 2 tbsp hot water*
*70 g/2½ oz pecan nuts, finely ground*
*1–2 tbsp chopped pecan nuts, to decorate*

**FROSTING**

*450 g/1 lb full-fat soft cheese*
*2 tbsp maple syrup*
*115 g/4 oz icing sugar*

*1.* Preheat the oven to 180°C/350°F/Gas Mark 4. Grease three 23-cm/9-inch round sandwich tins and line the bases with baking paper.

*2.* Sift together the flour and baking powder into a large bowl. Add the butter, sugar, eggs and coffee and beat with a hand-held electric mixer for 1–2 minutes until creamy. Fold in the nuts.

*3.* Divide the mixture between the prepared tins and smooth the surfaces with a palette knife. Bake in the preheated oven for 20–25 minutes until risen, golden and just firm to the touch. Leave the cakes to cool in the tins for 10 minutes, then turn out onto a wire rack and leave to cool completely.

*4.* To make the frosting, put the cheese and maple syrup into a bowl and beat together to blend. Sift in the sugar and beat until smooth.

*5.* Sandwich the cakes together with one third of the frosting. Spread the remainder over the top and side of the cake and decorate with the chopped pecan nuts.

# BLUEBERRY TRAY BAKE

**SERVES:** *12* | **PREP:** *30–35 mins, plus cooling* | **COOK:** *40 mins*

**INGREDIENTS**

*250 g/9 oz plain flour, plus extra for dusting*
*1 tsp baking powder*
*175 g/6 oz butter, softened, plus extra for greasing*
*85 g/3 oz caster sugar*
*1 egg, beaten*

**TOPPING**

*2 eggs*
*150 ml/5 fl oz whipping cream*
*55 g/2 oz caster sugar*
*4 tbsp blueberry jam*
*200 g/7 oz fresh blueberries*

*1.* Preheat the oven to 180°C/350°F/Gas Mark 4. Grease a 23 x 33-cm/9 x 13-inch Swiss roll tin and line with baking paper.

*2.* Sift the flour and baking powder into a large bowl and add the butter. Rub the butter into the flour until it resembles coarse breadcrumbs. Stir in the sugar and egg and beat until the mixture starts to clump together.

*3.* Gather the mixture together and lightly knead on a floured surface. Press out in an even layer in the base of the prepared tin, using floured hands. Prick the mixture all over with the prongs of a fork.

*4.* Bake in the preheated oven for 15 minutes, or until golden and springy to the touch. Leave to cool slightly in the tin. Do not switch off the oven.

*5.* To make the topping, place the eggs, cream and sugar in a bowl and whisk until smooth.

*6.* Spread the jam over the base, then gently spoon over the egg mixture. Scatter over the blueberries and return to the oven for 25 minutes, or until the topping is set and the cake is golden. Cut into slices and serve warm or cold.

# ANGEL FOOD CAKE

**SERVES:** *12* | **PREP:** *25–30 mins* | **COOK:** *35–45 mins*

**NGREDIENTS**

*tbsp sunflower oil, for oiling*
*large egg whites*
*tsp cream of tartar*
*tsp almond extract*
*50 g/9 oz caster sugar*
*15 g/4 oz plain flour, plus extra for dusting*

**ECORATION**

*50 g/9 oz summer berries*
*tbsp lemon juice*
*tbsp icing sugar*

*1.* Preheat the oven to 160°C/325°F/Gas Mark 3. Oil a 24-cm/9½-inch ring tin and lightly dust with flour.

*2.* Whisk the egg whites in a clean, grease-free bowl until they hold soft peaks. Add the cream of tartar and whisk again until the whites are stiff but not dry. Whisk in the almond extract, then add the caster sugar, a tablespoon at a time, whisking hard between each addition. Sift in the flour and fold in lightly and evenly using a large metal spoon.

*3.* Spoon the mixture into the prepared tin. Bake in the preheated oven for 40–45 minutes, or until golden brown. Run the tip of a knife around the edges of the cake to loosen from the tin. Leave to cool in the tin for 10 minutes, then turn out onto a wire rack and leave to cool completely.

*4.* To make the decoration, place the berries, lemon juice and icing sugar in a saucepan and heat until the sugar has dissolved. Spoon over the cake.

# FESTIVE CHOCOLATE & CHESTNUT ROULADE

**SERVES:** *6* | **PREP:** *45 mins* | **COOK:** *20 mins, plus cooling*

**INGREDIENTS**

*6 large eggs, separated*
*150 g/5½ oz caster sugar*
*½ tsp vanilla extract or chocolate extract*
*50 g/1¾ oz cocoa powder*
*icing sugar, for dusting*
*250 ml/9 fl oz double cream*
*250 g/9 oz sweetened chestnut purée*
*2 tbsp brandy*
*70 g/2½ oz cooked peeled chestnuts, chopped*

*1.* Preheat the oven to 180°C/350°F/Gas Mark 4. Line a 23 x 45-cm/9 x 17¾-inch Swiss roll tin with baking paper.

*2.* Using a hand-held electric mixer, beat together the egg yolks, caster sugar and vanilla extract in a bowl for 10 minutes, or until doubled in volume and pale and fluffy. In a separate bowl, whisk the egg whites until they hold soft peaks. Fold a tablespoon of egg whites into the egg yolk mixture, then gently fold in the remaining egg whites and the cocoa powder.

*3.* Spoon the mixture into the prepared tin and smooth the surface with a palette knife. Bake in the preheated oven for 20 minutes, or until risen and springy to the touch. Leave to cool in the tin.

*4.* Place a large piece of baking paper on a clean tea towel and dust with icing sugar. Invert the sponge onto the baking paper and carefully peel away the lining paper. In a clean bowl, whisk the cream until it holds stiff peaks, then stir in the chestnut purée and brandy. Spread over the sponge, leaving a 2.5-cm/1-inch margin, and scatter over the chestnuts. Using one end of the tea towel, carefully roll up the roulade. Dust with icing sugar and serve.

# DAIRY-FREE MIXED BERRY BUNDT CAKE

**SERVES:** *12* | **PREP:** *15–20 mins* | **COOK:** *1 hour–1 hour 5 mins, plus cooling*

**INGREDIENTS**

*1 tbsp rapeseed oil, for oiling*
*350 g/12 oz plain flour, plus extra for dusting*
*2 tsp baking powder*
*1 tsp bicarbonate of soda*
*400 g/14 oz caster sugar*
*55 g/2 oz desiccated coconut*
*500 ml/17 fl oz soya milk*
*150 ml/5 fl oz rapeseed oil*
*2 tsp vanilla extract*
*1 tsp salt*
*250 g/9 oz mixed berries, such as raspberries, blueberries and blackberries*
*icing sugar, for dusting*

*1.* Preheat the oven to 180°C/350°F/Gas Mark 4. Grease a 24-cm/9½-inch bundt tin and dust with flour.

*2.* Sift together the flour, baking powder and bicarbonate of soda into a large bowl and stir in the sugar and coconut. Add the soya milk, oil and vanilla extract. Beat together until smooth and thick. Stir in the salt and berries.

*3.* Pour the batter into the prepared tin and bake in the preheated oven for 1 hour, or until a skewer inserted into the centre of the cake comes out clean. Leave to cool in the tin for 5 minutes, then turn out onto a wire rack and leave to cool completely.

*4.* Dust the cake with icing sugar, slice and serve.

CHAPTER TWO

# SMALL CAKES & BARS

# APPLE SAUCE SPICED CUPCAKES

**MAKES:** *12* | **PREP:** *40 mins* | **COOK:** *1 hour 15 mins, plus cooling*

**INGREDIENTS**

*3 dessert apples*
*finely grated zest and juice of 1 unwaxed lemon*
*85 g/3 oz plain wholemeal flour*
*85 g/3 oz brown rice flour*
*2 tsp baking powder*
*½ tsp mixed spice, plus extra to decorate*
*115 g/4 oz unsalted butter, softened and diced*
*115 g/4 oz light muscovado sugar*
*2 eggs, beaten*
*225 ml/8 fl oz crème fraîche*

*1.* Peel, core and roughly chop two of the apples, then put them in a saucepan. Add the lemon zest and half the lemon juice, cover and cook over a medium–low heat for 5–10 minutes, or until soft. Mash until smooth, then leave to cool. Preheat the oven to 180°C/350°F/Gas Mark 4.

*2.* Put 12 paper cases or squares of baking paper in a 12-hole muffin tin. Put the wholemeal flour, rice flour, baking powder and mixed spice in a small bowl and mix well.

*3.* Cream together the butter and sugar in a large bowl. Gradually add the eggs, alternating with the flour mixture until it is all used up, then stir in 150 g/5½ oz of the apple sauce.

*4.* Spoon the mixture into the paper cases. Bake in the preheated oven for 15–18 minutes, or until well risen and springy to the touch. Leave to cool in the tin for 5 minutes, then turn out and transfer to a wire rack.

*5.* Line a baking sheet with baking paper. Put the remaining lemon juice in a medium-sized bowl. Thinly slice the remaining apple, toss in the lemon juice, then arrange on the prepared baking sheet in a single layer. Reduce the oven temperature to 110°C/225°F/Gas Mark ¼ and cook the apple slices, turning once, for 30–45 minutes, or until just beginning to brown. Switch off the oven and leave the apples inside it to cool. Lift off the slices with a palette knife and cut them in half.

*6.* Top each cupcake with a spoonful of crème fraîche, sprinkle with mixed spice and place two apple slice halves on top.

# RASPBERRY JAM CUPCAKES

**MAKES:** *28* | **PREP:** *25 mins* | **COOK:** *15–20 mins, plus cooling*

**INGREDIENTS**

*175 g/6 oz plain flour*
*1 tbsp baking powder*
*1 tbsp custard powder*
*175 g/6 oz butter, softened*
*175 g/6 oz golden caster sugar*
*3 eggs, beaten*
*1 tsp vanilla extract*
*70 g/2½ oz raspberry jam*
*icing sugar, for dusting*

*1.* Preheat the oven to 190°C/375°F/Gas Mark 5. Line several bun tins with 28 paper cases.

*2.* Sift the flour, baking powder and custard powder into a large bowl and add the butter, caster sugar, eggs and vanilla extract. Beat well until smooth.

*3.* Divide the mixture between the paper cases and place ½ teaspoon of jam into the centre of each, without pressing down.

*4.* Bake in the preheated oven for 15–20 minutes, or until risen, golden and springy to the touch. Leave to cool in the tins for 5 minutes, then transfer to a wire rack and leave to cool completely. Dust with icing sugar and serve.

# CLASSIC VANILLA CUPCAKES

**MAKES:** *12* | **PREP:** *25 mins* | **COOK:** *15–20 mins, plus cooling*

**INGREDIENTS**

*175 g/6 oz unsalted butter, softened*
*175 g/6 oz caster sugar*
*3 large eggs, beaten*
*1 tsp vanilla extract*
*175 g/6 oz self-raising flour*

**FROSTING**

*150 g/5½ oz unsalted butter, softened*
*3 tbsp double cream*
*1 tsp vanilla extract*
*300 g/10½ oz icing sugar, sifted*
*hundreds and thousands, to decorate*

*1.* Preheat the oven to 180°C/350°F/Gas Mark 4. Line a 12-hole bun tin with paper cases.

*2.* Put the butter and caster sugar into a bowl and cream together until light and fluffy. Gradually beat in the eggs and vanilla extract. Sift in the flour and fold in gently.

*3.* Divide the mixture between the paper cases and bake in the preheated oven for 15–20 minutes, or until risen and firm to the touch. Transfer to a wire rack and leave to cool.

*4.* To make the frosting, put the butter into a bowl and beat with a hand-held electric mixer for 2–3 minutes, or until pale and creamy. Beat in the cream and vanilla extract. Gradually beat in the icing sugar and continue beating until the buttercream is light and fluffy.

*5.* Use a palette knife to swirl the frosting over the tops of the cupcakes. Decorate with hundreds and thousands and serve.

# CHOCOLATE BUTTERFLY CUPCAKES

**MAKES:** *12* | **PREP:** *25 mins* | **COOK:** *15 mins, plus cooling*

**NGREDIENTS**

*25 g/4½ oz soft margarine*
*25 g/4½ oz caster sugar*
*50 g/5½ oz self-raising flour, sifted*
*large eggs*
*tbsp cocoa powder*
*5 g/1 oz plain chocolate, melted*

**EMON BUTTERCREAM**

*00 g/3½ oz unsalted butter, softened*
*25 g/8 oz icing sugar, sifted, plus extra for dusting*
*inely grated rind of 1 lemon*
*tbsp lemon juice*

*1.* Preheat the oven to 180°C/350°F/Gas Mark 4. Line a 12-hole bun tin with paper cases.

*2.* Place the margarine, caster sugar, flour, eggs and cocoa powder in a large bowl and beat until just smooth. Add the chocolate and beat.

*3.* Spoon the mixture into the paper cases, filling them three-quarters full, and bake in the preheated oven for 15 minutes, or until well risen. Transfer to a wire rack and leave to cool completely.

*4.* To make the buttercream, place the butter in a mixing bowl and beat until fluffy. Gradually add the icing sugar, lemon rind and lemon juice, beating well after each addition.

*5.* Cut the top off each cake, using a serrated knife. Cut each cake top in half. Spread the lemon buttercream over the cut surface of each cake and push the two pieces of cake top into the icing to form wings. Dust with icing sugar and serve.

# SWEET POTATO, COCONUT & LIME CUPCAKES

**MAKES:** *18* | **PREP:** *20–25 mins, plus cooling* | **COOK:** *1 hour–1 hour 5 mins*

**INGREDIENTS**

*2 sweet potatoes*
*175 g/6 oz spelt flour*
*2 tsp baking powder*
*½ tsp bicarbonate of soda*
*½ tsp ground ginger*
*¼ tsp salt*
*150 g/5½ oz golden caster sugar*
*115 g/4 oz solid coconut oil*
*2 large eggs*

**FROSTING**

*225 g/8 oz unsalted butter, diced, at room temperature*
*325 g/11½ oz icing sugar, sifted*
*2 x 50-g/1¾-oz sachets creamed coconut, melted*
*½ tsp vanilla extract*
*⅛ tsp salt*
*½ tbsp finely grated lime rind*
*1 tbsp lime juice*
*3 tbsp toasted coconut flakes, to decorate*
*3 tbsp lime rind slivers, to decorate*

*1.* Preheat the oven to 220°C/425°F/Gas Mark 7. Place the sweet potatoes on a baking tray and bake in the preheated oven for 45 minutes. Peel when cool enough to handle and purée in a food processor until smooth. Set aside until needed.

*2.* Reduce the oven temperature to 180°C/350°F/Gas Mark 4. Line two 9-hole bun tins with paper cases.

*3.* Sift together the flour, baking powder, bicarbonate of soda, ginger and salt twice into a bowl.

*4.* Put the sugar and oil into a separate bowl and beat with a hand-held electric mixer for 3 minutes until light and fluffy. Beat in the eggs one at a time, alternating with the flour mixture, beating well after each addition. Stir in the sweet potato purée.

*5.* Spoon the mixture into the paper cases, filling them about two-thirds full. Bake in the preheated oven for 15–20 minutes, turning the tins halfway through the cooking time, until a skewer inserted into the centre comes out clean. Leave to cool in the tins for 10 minutes, then transfer to a wire rack and leave to cool completely.

*6.* To make the frosting, put the butter and icing sugar into a bowl and beat with a hand-held electric mixer for 1 minute, or until fluffy. Beat in the remaining ingredients.

*7.* Swirl the frosting onto the cupcakes. Decorate with toasted coconut flakes and thin slivers of lime and serve.

# VEGAN & GLUTEN-FREE COOKIES & CREAM CUPCAKES

**MAKES:** *12* | **PREP:** *20 mins* | **COOK:** *18–20 mins, plus cooling*

**INGREDIENTS**

*250 ml/9 fl oz gluten-free soya milk*
*1 tsp vegan and gluten-free cider vinegar*
*150 g/5½ oz caster sugar*
*75 ml/2½ fl oz rapeseed oil*
*1 tsp vanilla extract*
*150 g/5½ oz gluten-free plain flour*
*25 g/1 oz vegan and gluten-free cocoa powder*
*¾ tsp gluten-free bicarbonate of soda*
*½ tsp gluten-free baking powder*
*70 g/2½ oz vegan and gluten-free cookies, finely chopped*

**TOPPING**

*35 g/1¼ oz vegan and gluten-free margarine*
*35 g/1¼ oz white vegetable shortening*
*300 g/10½ oz vegan and gluten-free icing sugar*
*¼ tsp vanilla extract*
*75 ml/2½ fl oz gluten-free soya cream*
*35 g/1¼ oz vegan and gluten-free cookies, finely chopped*

*1.* Preheat the oven to 180°C/350°F/Gas Mark 4. Line a 12-hole bun tin with paper cases.

*2.* Put the milk into a measuring jug, stir in the vinegar and set aside for a few minutes to curdle.

*3.* Put the sugar, oil and vanilla extract into a large mixing bowl and beat together. Pour in the milk and vinegar mixture and mix thoroughly, then add the flour, cocoa powder, bicarbonate of soda and baking powder. Stir until the ingredients are just combined, then fold in the cookie crumbs.

*4.* Divide the mixture between the paper cases and bake in the preheated oven for 18–20 minutes, or until golden and springy to the touch. Transfer to a wire rack and leave to cool completely.

*5.* To make the topping, beat the margarine and vegetable shortening together, then mix in the icing sugar and the vanilla extract. Gradually add the cream until you have a thick pipeable consistency. Generously pipe or spoon the icing over the cupcakes, sprinkle with cookie crumbs and serve.

# WHITE CHOCOLATE & BLACKBERRY MUFFINS

**MAKES:** *12* | **PREP:** *10–15 mins* | **COOK:** *25–30 mins*

**INGREDIENTS**

*300 g/10½ oz plain flour*
*1 tsp baking powder*
*200 g/7 oz caster sugar*
*100 g/3½ oz unsalted butter*
*2 eggs*
*1 tbsp vanilla extract*
*250 g/9 oz low-fat natural yogurt*
*200 g/7 oz blackberries*
*200 g/7 oz white chocolate, chopped into chunks*

*1.* Preheat the oven to 180°C/350°F/Gas Mark 4. Line a 12-hole muffin tin with paper cases.

*2.* Sift together the flour, baking powder and sugar into a large bowl. In a separate bowl beat together the butter, eggs, vanilla extract and yogurt until combined.

*3.* Fold the egg mixture into the flour mixture until just combined. Stir in the blackberries and chocolate.

*4.* Divide the mixture between the paper cases and bake in the preheated oven for 25–30 minutes until golden, cooked through and springy to the touch. Transfer to a wire rack and leave to cool.

# LOW-FAT PUMPKIN PIE MUFFINS

**MAKES:** *10* | **PREP:** *20–25 mins* | **COOK:** *25 mins*

**INGREDIENTS**

*325 g/11½ oz plain wholemeal flour*
*125 g/4½ oz oatmeal*
*1¼ tsp baking powder*
*1¼ tsp bicarbonate of soda*
*¼ tsp salt*
*2 tsp mixed spice*
*60 g/2¼ oz molasses sugar*
*1 tbsp stevia granules*
*2 egg whites*
*2 tsp vanilla extract*
*275 g/9¾ oz cooked pumpkin flesh, mashed until smooth (about 325 g/11½ oz uncooked weight)*
*1½ tbsp groundnut oil*
*100 g/3½ oz unsweetened apple sauce*
*250 ml/9 fl oz unsweetened vanilla almond milk*

*1.* Preheat the oven to 180°C/350°F/Gas Mark 4. Line ten holes in a 12-hole muffin tin with paper cases.

*2.* Put the flour, oatmeal, baking powder, bicarbonate of soda, salt and mixed spice into a large bowl and mix well together.

*3.* Beat together the sugar, stevia granules, egg whites and vanilla extract in a mixing bowl, then beat in the pumpkin, oil, apple sauce and almond milk. Add the flour mixture and beat until just mixed.

*4.* Divide the mixture between the paper cases. Bake in the preheated oven for 25 minutes, or until a skewer inserted into the centre of a muffin comes out clean.

*5.* Leave the muffins in the tin until cool enough to handle, then transfer to a wire rack and leave to cool completely. They are best eaten within 24 hours but will store for a little longer, and will freeze for up to 1 month.

# GLUTEN-FREE BANANA MUFFINS WITH MAPLE CREAM FROSTING

**MAKES:** *12* | **PREP:** *20–25 mins* | **COOK:** *20–25 mins, plus cooling*

**INGREDIENTS**

*125 g/4¼ oz butter*
*160 g/5¾ oz soft light brown sugar*
*2 eggs*
*125 ml/4 fl oz single cream*
*2 tbsp maple syrup*
*1 tbsp glycerine*
*225 g/8 oz gluten-free self raising flour, sifted*
*½ tsp gluten-free bicarbonate of soda*
*425 g/15 oz bananas, mashed*

**FROSTING**

*55 g/2 oz butter, softened*
*125 g/4½ oz cream cheese*
*375 g/13 oz gluten-free icing sugar*
*4 tbsp maple syrup, plus extra to serve (optional)*

*1.* Preheat the oven to 180°C/350°F/Gas 4. Line a 12-hole muffin in with paper cases.

*2.* Put the butter and brown sugar into a food processor and process until light and fluffy. Add the eggs, then slowly mix in the cream, maple syrup, glycerine, flour and bicarbonate of soda. Fold in the mashed bananas and process to combine.

*3.* Divide the mixture between the paper cases and bake in the preheated oven for 25–30 minutes until well-risen and golden. Remove from the oven, transfer to a wire rack and leave to cool.

*4.* To make the frosting, put the butter, cream cheese, icing sugar and maple syrup into a food processor and process until pale and fluffy.

*5.* Place the frosting in a piping bag fitted with a star nozzle and pipe some onto each muffin. Serve with maple syrup, if using.

2
3
5

# DOUBLE CHOCOLATE PISTACHIO BROWNIES

**MAKES:** *12* | **PREP:** *20–25 mins, plus cooling* | **COOK:** *40–45 mins*

**INGREDIENTS**

*225 g/8 oz butter, softened, plus extra for greasing*
*150 g/5½ oz plain chocolate, broken into pieces*
*225 g/8 oz self-raising flour*
*125 g/4½ oz caster sugar*
*4 eggs, beaten*
*75 g/2¾ oz pistachio nuts, chopped*
*100 g/3½ oz white chocolate, roughly chopped*
*sifted icing sugar, for dusting*

*1.* Preheat the oven to 180°C/350°F/Gas Mark 4. Grease a 23-cm/9-inch square baking tin and line with baking paper.

*2.* Place the plain chocolate and the butter in a heatproof bowl set over a saucepan of gently simmering water and heat, stirring, until melted, then leave to cool slightly.

*3.* Sift the flour into a separate bowl and stir in the caster sugar.

*4.* Stir the eggs into the chocolate mixture, then pour into the flour and sugar mixture and beat well. Add the nuts and white chocolate and stir to combine.

*5.* Pour the mixture into the prepared tin, using a palette knife to spread it evenly.

*6.* Bake in the preheated oven for 30–35 minutes, or until firm to the touch around the edges. Leave to cool in the tin for 20 minutes, then turn out onto a wire rack.

*7.* Dust with icing sugar and leave to cool completely, then cut into 12 squares and serve.

# LOW-SUGAR BLACK BEAN BROWNIES

**MAKES:** *16* | **PREP:** *25 mins, plus cooling* | **COOK:** *35 mins*

**NGREDIENTS**

*00 g/3½ oz plain chocolate chips, 70% cocoa solids*
*tbsp coconut oil*
*75 g/13 oz black beans in water, drained*
*75 g/6 oz Medjool dates, halved and stoned*
*eggs*
*0 g/2½ oz light muscovado sugar*
*tsp natural vanilla extract*
*5 g/2 oz cocoa powder*
*½ tsp baking powder*
*tsp ground cinnamon*
*tsp sea salt*

*1.* Preheat the oven to 180°C/350°F/Gas Mark 4. Line a 20-cm/8-inch shallow square cake tin with a single piece of non-stick baking paper, cutting into the corners to make it fit.

*2.* Add 55 g/2 oz of the chocolate chips to a small saucepan with the oil and heat over a very low heat until the oil has melted, then remove and leave to stand for a few minutes until the chocolate has melted completely.

*3.* Meanwhile, add the beans and dates to a food processor or blender and process to a coarse purée. Add the eggs, sugar, vanilla extract, chocolate and coconut oil mixture, and process until smooth.

*4.* Mix the cocoa powder, baking powder, cinnamon and salt together, then add to the bean mixture and process until smooth.

*5.* Spoon into the prepared tin and spread in an even layer. Bake in the preheated oven for about 25 minutes, or until the cake is well risen, beginning to crack around the edges and still slightly soft in the centre

*6.* Sprinkle with the remaining chocolate chips and leave to cool for 20 minutes. Use the paper to lift the cake out of the tin, transfer to a wire rack and leave to cool completely. Cut into 16 small pieces, remove from the paper and store in a tin for up to 2 days.

# RHUBARB & LEMON DRIZZLE SQUARES

**MAKES:** *9* | **PREP:** *30–35 mins, plus cooling* | **COOK:** *35–40 mins*

**INGREDIENTS**

*300 g/10½ oz trimmed young rhubarb, cut into 2-cm/¾-inch thick slices*
*100 g/3½ oz ground almonds*
*115 g/4 oz brown rice flour*
*1½ tsp baking powder*
*1 ripe banana, mashed*
*150 ml/5 fl oz rice bran oil*
*115 g/4 oz light muscovado sugar*
*grated zest of 1 lemon*
*3 eggs*
*25 g/1 oz unblanched almonds, roughly chopped*

**SYRUP**

*juice of 2 lemons*
*60 g/2¼ oz light muscovado sugar*

*1.* Preheat the oven to 180°C/350°F/Gas Mark 4. Line a 30 x 20 x 4-cm/12 x 8 x 1½-inch square cake tin with a single piece of non-stick baking paper, cutting into the corners to make it fit.

*2.* Place the rhubarb in a roasting tin and bake in the preheated oven for 10 minutes until almost soft. Remove from the oven but do not switch off the oven.

*3.* Put the ground almonds, flour and baking powder into a bowl and stir together until combined.

*4.* Put the banana, oil, sugar and lemon zest into a separate bowl and beat until smooth. Beat in the eggs, one at a time, then beat in the flour mixture.

*5.* Spoon the batter into the prepared tin, then scatter the rhubarb over the top. Bake for 25–30 minutes, until the cake is well risen and springy to the touch.

*6.* Meanwhile, to make the syrup, mix the lemon juice with the sugar. Spoon half over the hot cake and leave to soak in for 1–2 minutes. Spoon over the remaining syrup, scatter with the chopped almonds and leave to cool in the tin.

*7.* Lift the cake out of the tin, peel away the paper and cut the cake into 9 squares. Eat within 2 days or freeze until needed.

2

4

6

2

3

4

# CHOCOLATE CARAMEL SHORTBREAD

**MAKES:** *12* | **PREP:** *20 mins, plus chilling* | **COOK:** *35–45 mins*

**GREDIENTS**

*5 g/4 oz butter, plus extra for greasing*
*75 g/6 oz plain flour*
*5 g/2 oz golden caster sugar*

**LLING AND TOPPING**

*75 g/6 oz butter*
*5 g/4 oz golden caster sugar*
*tbsp golden syrup*
*0 ml/14 fl oz canned condensed milk*
*0 g/7 oz plain chocolate, broken into pieces*

*1.* Preheat the oven to 180°C/350°F/Gas Mark 4. Grease a 23-cm/9-inch shallow square cake tin and line with baking paper.

*2.* Put the butter, flour and sugar into a food processor and process until the mixture begins to bind together. Press into the prepared tin and smooth the top. Bake in the preheated oven for 20–25 minutes, or until golden.

*3.* Meanwhile, make the filling. Place the butter, sugar, golden syrup and condensed milk in a saucepan and gently heat until the sugar has dissolved. Bring to the boil and simmer for 6–8 minutes, stirring constantly, until very thick. Pour over the shortbread base and chill in the refrigerator for 30 minutes, or until firm.

*4.* To make the topping, put the chocolate into a heatproof bowl set over a saucepan of gently simmering water and heat until melted, then spread it over the caramel. Chill in the refrigerator until set. Cut the shortbread into 12 pieces with a sharp knife and serve.

# WHITE CHOCOLATE & LEMON SQUARES

**MAKES:** *9* | **PREP:** *20 mins, plus cooling & setting* | **COOK:** *1 hour–1 hour 5 mins*

**IGREDIENTS**

*)0 g/3½ oz unsalted butter, plus extra for greasing*
*)0 g/6½ oz caster sugar*
*50 g/5½ oz plain flour*
*inch of salt*
*tsp vanilla extract*
*eggs*
*tbsp lemon zest*
*)0 ml/3½ fl oz lemon juice*
*)0 g/3½ oz white chocolate*
*5 g/1 oz plain chocolate*
*fresh raspberries*

*1.* Preheat the oven to 180°C/350°F/Gas Mark 4. Grease a 20-cm/8-inch square baking tin and line with baking paper.

*2.* Place the butter, 50 g/1¾ oz of the sugar, 125 g/4½ oz of the flour and the salt in a food processor and pulse until fine and grainy. Add the vanilla extract and pulse until the mixture comes together.

*3.* Turn out into the prepared tin and press down evenly with the back of a spoon. Transfer to the preheated oven and bake for 16–18 minutes until lightly browned.

*4.* Meanwhile, whisk together the eggs, the remaining sugar, the lemon zest, lemon juice and the remaining flour until smooth and combined. Pour over the base and return to the oven for 30 minutes until the filling is set. Leave to cool in the tin.

*5.* Put the white chocolate into a heatproof bowl set over a saucepan of gently simmering water and heat until melted. Leave to cool slightly before pouring over the cake. Leave to set.

*6.* Put the plain chocolate into a separate heatproof bowl set over a saucepan of gently simmering water and heat until melted. Drizzle over the cake. Leave to set, then cut the cake into 9 squares, place a raspberry on top of each square and serve.

2
3
4

# LEMON POPPY SEED MADELEINES

**MAKES:** *36* | **PREP:** *20 mins* | **COOK:** *10 mins*

**NGREDIENTS**

*unflower oil, for oiling*
*eggs*
*egg yolk*
*nely grated rind of 1 lemon*
*40 g/5 oz golden caster sugar*
*40 g/5 oz plain flour*
*tsp baking powder*
*40 g/5 oz unsalted butter, melted and cooled*
*tbsp poppy seeds*

*1.* Preheat the oven to 190°C/375°F/Gas Mark 5. Lightly oil three 12-hole madeleine tins.

*2.* Whisk together the eggs, egg yolk, lemon rind and sugar in a large bowl until very pale and thick.

*3.* Sift together the flour and baking powder into the mixture and lightly fold in using a metal spoon. Fold in the melted butter and poppy seeds.

*4.* Spoon the mixture into the prepared tins and bake in the preheated oven for about 10 minutes until well risen.

*5.* Turn out the cakes onto a wire rack and leave to cool, then serve very fresh.

# MINI VICTORIA SANDWICH CAKES

**MAKES:** *12* | **PREP:** *35–40 mins, plus cooling* | **COOK:** *15 mins*

**INGREDIENTS**

*70 g/2½ oz butter, softened, plus extra for greasing*
*70 g/2½ oz caster sugar*
*70 g/2½ oz self-raising flour*
*1 egg*
*1 egg yolk*
*1 tsp vanilla extract*

**TO DECORATE**

*150 ml/5 fl oz double cream*
*6 tbsp strawberry jam*
*85 g/3 oz icing sugar*
*1 tbsp lemon juice*

*1.* Preheat the oven to 180°C/350°F/Gas Mark 4. Grease a 12-hole mini muffin tin.

*2.* Place the butter, caster sugar, flour, egg, egg yolk and vanilla extract in a large bowl and beat with a hand-held electric mixer until smooth and creamy.

*3.* Using a teaspoon, spoon the mixture evenly into the prepared tin. Bake in the preheated oven for 15 minutes, or until risen, golden and springy to the touch. Leave to cool slightly, then transfer to a wire rack and leave to cool completely.

*4.* To decorate, whip the cream until it holds soft peaks. Split the cakes in half horizontally using a small serrated knife. Press 2 tablespoons of the jam through a small sieve into a bowl to extract the seeds. Put the sieved jam in a small paper piping bag and snip off the tip. Sandwich the cakes together with the remaining jam and cream.

*5.* Beat the icing sugar and lemon juice together in a bowl until smooth. Spoon the icing over the cakes, spreading it just to the edges. Pipe dots of jam on top of each cake and draw a wooden skewer through them.

4

4

5

# BERRY & RHUBARB CHEESECAKE BARS

**MAKES:** *8* | **PREP:** *15–20 mins* | **COOK:** *40–42 mins, plus cooling & chilling*

**INGREDIENTS**

*70 g/2½ oz digestive biscuits*
*1 tbsp soft light brown sugar*
*15 g/½ oz unsalted butter, melted, plus extra for greasing*
*1 tsp water*
*115 g/4 oz fresh mixed berries (blackberries, blueberries, strawberries or raspberries, diced if large)*
*125 g/4½ oz fresh rhubarb, diced*

**FILLING**

*225 g/8 oz cream cheese*
*55 g/2 oz honey*
*2 eggs, lightly beaten*
*1 tsp vanilla extract*
*1 tsp grated lemon rind*

*1.* Preheat the oven to 180°C/350°F/Gas Mark 4. Grease a 20-cm/8-inch square baking tin.

*2.* Pulse the biscuits and sugar in a food processor until coarsely ground. Add the butter and water and whizz until moist. Press the mixture into the prepared tin in an even layer, and bake in the preheated oven for about 10–12 minutes, or until it begins to colour. Remove from the oven and leave to cool while you prepare the filling. Do not switch off the oven.

*3.* To make the filling, beat together the cream cheese and honey with a hand-held electric mixer until smooth. Add the eggs, vanilla extract and lemon rind and beat until fluffy.

*4.* Spread the cream cheese mixture on top of the base in an even layer. Sprinkle the berries and rhubarb evenly over the top. Bake for about 30 minutes, or until the filling is almost set. Remove from the oven and leave to cool to room temperature, then chill in the refrigerator for about 2 hours.

*5.* Slice into 8 bars and serve chilled.

# VEGAN & GLUTEN-FREE PEANUT BUTTER GRANOLA BARS

**MAKES:** *12* | **PREP:** *15 mins* | **COOK:** *25 mins, plus cooling*

**INGREDIENTS**

*vegan and gluten-free margarine, for greasing*
*100 g/3½ oz crunchy peanut butter*
*25 g/1 oz soft light brown sugar*
*2 tbsp golden syrup*
*450 g/1 lb gluten-free granola*

*1.* Preheat the oven to 180°C/350°F/Gas Mark 4. Grease an 18 x 25-cm/7 x 10-inch shallow baking tin and line with baking paper. Cut the paper a little larger than necessary so that the edges are above the edges of the tin, as this will make it easier to lift the bars out.

*2.* Cream together the peanut butter, sugar and golden syrup with a hand-held electric mixer or a wooden spoon. Stir in the granola and mix well. Put the mixture into the prepared tin and use the back of a metal spoon to press it into a smooth layer.

*3.* Bake in the preheated oven for 25 minutes, or until golden brown. Carefully lift the baked mixture out of the tin by holding the edges of the baking paper. Leaving the paper underneath for support, place on a wire rack and leave to cool completely, then use a sharp knife to cut into 12 bars.

2

3

4

# GINGER & CHOCOLATE FLAPJACKS

**MAKES:** *12* | **PREP:** *10 mins* | **COOK:** *25–30 mins, plus chilling*

**INGREDIENTS**

*175 g/6 oz butter, plus extra for greasing*
*115 g/4 oz soft light brown sugar*
*3 tbsp golden syrup*
*1 tbsp stem ginger syrup*
*2 pieces stem ginger, finely chopped*
*350 g/12 oz rolled oats*

**CHOCOLATE GLAZE**

*175 g/6 oz plain chocolate, broken into pieces*
*40 g/1½ oz butter*

*1.* Preheat the oven to 180°C/350°F/Gas Mark 4. Grease a 28 x 18-cm/11 x 7-inch shallow baking tin.

*2.* Put the butter, sugar, golden syrup and stem ginger syrup into a large saucepan over a low heat and heat gently until melted. Remove from the heat and stir in the ginger and oats.

*3.* Spoon the mixture into the prepared tin and smooth the surface. Bake in the preheated oven for 15–20 minutes, or until pale golden. Leave to cool in the tin.

*4.* Meanwhile, to make the glaze, put the chocolate and butter into a heatproof bowl set over a saucepan of gently simmering water and heat until melted. Stir until smooth, then spread over the cooled flapjacks. Chill in the refrigerator for 1 hour, or until set. Cut into 12 bars and serve.

# APPLE STREUSEL BARS

**MAKES:** *14* | **PREP:** *15 mins* | **COOK:** *45–55 mins*

**INGREDIENTS**

*2 eating apples, peeled, cored and diced*
*2 tbsp lemon juice*
*125 g/4½ oz unsalted butter, softened, plus extra for greasing*
*125 g/4½ oz golden caster sugar*
*1 tsp vanilla extract*
*2 eggs, beaten*
*150 g/5½ oz self-raising flour*

**TOPPING**

*40 g/1½ oz blanched almonds, finely chopped*
*40 g/1½ oz oz plain flour*
*40 g/1½ oz oz light muscovado sugar*
*½ tsp ground cinnamon*
*25 g/1 oz unsalted butter, melted*

*1.* Preheat the oven to 180°C/350°F/ Gas Mark 4. Grease and line a 28 x 18-cm/11 x 7-inch traybake tin. Sprinkle the apples with the lemon juice.

*2.* Cream together the butter, sugar and vanilla extract until pale and fluffy. Gradually add the eggs, beating thoroughly after each addition

*3.* Sift in the flour and fold in evenly, then stir in the apples. Spread evenly in the prepared tin.

*4.* To make the topping, mix all the ingredients together until coarse crumbs form, then sprinkle over the cake. Bake in the preheated oven for 45–55 minutes until firm and golden.

*5.* Cut into 14 bars and serve warm or cold.

2
3
4

# SALTED CARAMEL & CHOCOLATE BITES

**MAKES:** *20* | **PREP:** *30 mins* | **COOK:** *35–40 mins, plus cooling*

**INGREDIENTS**

*sunflower oil, for oiling*
*200 g/7 oz plain chocolate, roughly chopped*
*150 g/5½ oz unsalted butter*
*2 eggs*
*175 g/6 oz soft light brown sugar*
*55 g/2 oz plain flour*
*1 tsp baking powder*
*55 g/2 oz walnut pieces, roughly chopped*
*6 tbsp dulce de leche (caramel sauce)*
*1 tbsp sea salt*

*1.* Preheat the oven to 160°C/325°F/Gas Mark 3. Lightly oil a 20-cm/8-inch square baking tin and line with a single piece of non-stick baking paper, snipping into the corners to make it fit.

*2.* Put 70 g/2½ oz of the chocolate and all the butter in a heatproof bowl set over a saucepan of gently simmering water and heat until melted, stirring occasionally.

*3.* Put the eggs and sugar into a mixing bowl, then sift in the flour and baking powder. Stir in the melted chocolate mixture and beat together until blended. Add the walnuts and the remaining chocolate and stir together. Pour the mixture into the prepared tin and smooth the surface with a spatula.

*4.* Put the caramel into a small bowl and beat, then swirl it through the chocolate mixture using a fork. Scatter over the salt and bake in the preheated oven for 30–35 minutes, or until the cake begins to shrink slightly from the sides of the tin. Leave to cool for 1 hour.

*5.* Remove from the tin, peel off the paper and cut the cake into 20 small squares. Store in an airtight container in a cool, dry place for up to 2 days.

CHAPTER THREE

# COOKIES & BISCUITS

# RAINBOW SPRINKLE SUGAR COOKIES

**MAKES:** *18* | **PREP:** *25 mins, plus chilling* | **COOK:** *10–12 mins*

**INGREDIENTS**

*100 g/3½ oz unsalted butter, softened, plus extra for greasing*
*70 g/2½ oz caster sugar*
*100 g/3½ oz plain flour, plus extra for dusting*
*50 g/1¾ oz cornflour*
*1–2 tbsp milk*
*4 tbsp hundreds and thousands*

*1.* Put the butter and sugar into a large bowl and beat with a hand-held electric mixer until pale and creamy.

*2.* Sift in the flour and cornflour and mix to a crumbly dough. Gathe together with your hands and lightly knead on a floured surface until smooth. Wrap in clingfilm and chill in the refrigerator for 30 minutes.

*3.* Preheat the oven to 180°C/350°F/Gas Mark 4. Grease two large baking sheets.

*4.* Unwrap the dough and roll out between two large sheets of baking paper to a thickness of 5 mm/¼ inch. Using a 6-cm/2½-inc round fluted cutter, stamp out 18 cookies, re-rolling the trimmings as necessary.

*5.* Transfer the cookies to the prepared baking sheets. Lightly brush the tops with the milk and sprinkle liberally with the hundreds and thousands, gently pressing down with your fingertips.

*6.* Bake in the preheated oven for 10–12 minutes, or until pale golde Leave to cool on the baking sheets for a few minutes, then transfer wire racks and leave to cool completely.

1
2
4

1
2
3

# LEMON FORK COOKIES

**MAKES:** *16* | **PREP:** *15–20 mins* | **COOK:** *12–15 mins*

**NGREDIENTS**

*15 g/4 oz unsalted butter, softened, plus extra for greasing*
*5 g/2 oz caster sugar*
*nely grated rind of 1 small lemon*
*75 g/6 oz self-raising flour*

*1.* Preheat the oven to 180°C/350°F/Gas Mark 4. Lightly grease two large baking sheets. Put the butter into a large bowl and beat with a wooden spoon for 1 minute until very soft. Gradually beat in the sugar and lemon rind.

*2.* Sift in the flour and mix until crumbly. Gather together with your hands and lightly knead to a dough. Divide the dough into 16 pieces and shape each piece into a walnut-sized ball.

*3.* Place the balls on the prepared baking sheets, spaced well apart to allow for spreading. Dip the prongs of a fork into cold water, then use to flatten each ball of dough.

*4.* Bake in the preheated oven for 12–15 minutes, or until pale golden. Leave to cool on the baking sheets for 1–2 minutes, then transfer to a wire rack and leave to cool completely.

# CHOCOLATE CHIP COOKIES

**MAKES:** *20* | **PREP:** *25 mins, plus chilling & cooling* | **COOK:** *20 mins*

**INGREDIENTS**

*125 g/4½ oz butter, softened*
*75 g/2¾ oz soft light brown sugar*
*75 g/2¾ oz granulated sugar*
*½ tsp vanilla extract*
*1 egg*
*250 g/9 oz plain flour*
*½ tsp bicarbonate of soda*
*100 g/3½ oz chocolate chips*
*200 g/7 oz plain chocolate*
*50 ml/2 fl oz double cream*

*1.* Preheat the oven to 180°C/350°F/Gas Mark 4. Line three baking sheets with greaseproof paper or silicone sheets. Beat together the butter, brown sugar and granulated sugar until just combined. Add the vanilla extract and egg and beat until combined.

*2.* Sift the flour and bicarbonate of soda into a separate bowl, then gradually add to the butter mixture, mixing until just combined. Fold through the chocolate chips and bring the dough together with your hands. Wrap in clingfilm and chill in the refrigerator for 30 minutes.

*3.* Put the chocolate and cream into a heatproof bowl set over a saucepan of gently simmering water and heat until the chocolate is melted. Leave to cool for 15 minutes until just beginning to thicken.

*4.* Spoon the chocolate into a piping bag fitted with a 1-cm/½-inch round nozzle and set aside for 15 minutes, or until thick enough to pipe out chocolate drops. Pipe twenty 2 x 2-cm/¾ x ¾-inch mounds onto one of the prepared sheets. Chill in the refrigerator until hard.

*5.* Make 20 even-sized balls of cookie dough and place on the remaining prepared sheets, spaced well apart to allow for spreading. Bake in the preheated oven for 10 minutes until just golden but still slightly undercooked.

*6.* Leave the cookies to cool on the sheets for 15 minutes, then press a chocolate drop into the centre of each. Leave the cookies on the sheets to cool completely.

# WHITE CHOCOLATE & MACADAMIA NUT COOKIES

**MAKES:** *16* | **PREP:** *25 mins* | **COOK:** *12–14 mins*

**IGREDIENTS**

*15 g/4 oz butter, softened, plus extra for greasing*
*15 g/4 oz soft light brown sugar*
*tbsp golden syrup*
*75 g/6 oz self-raising flour*
*5 g/2 oz macadamia nuts, roughly chopped*
*5 g/2 oz white chocolate, chopped into chunks*

*1.* Preheat the oven to 180°C/350°F/Gas Mark 4. Grease two large baking sheets.

*2.* Put the butter and sugar into a bowl and cream together until light and fluffy, then beat in the golden syrup. Sift in the flour, add the nuts and mix to a rough dough.

*3.* Divide the dough into 16 even-sized balls and place on the prepared baking sheet, spaced well apart to allow for spreading. Slightly flatten each ball with your fingertips and top with the chocolate chunks, lightly pressing them into the dough.

*4.* Bake in the preheated oven for 12–14 minutes, or until just set and pale golden. Leave to cool on the baking sheets for 5 minutes, then transfer to a wire rack and leave to cool completely.

1
2
3

# MAPLE PECAN COOKIES

**MAKES:** *16* | **PREP:** *20 mins* | **COOK:** *12–14 mins*

**INGREDIENTS**

*70 g/2½ oz pecan nuts*
*115 g/4 oz butter, softened, plus extra for greasing*
*100 g/3½ oz dark muscovado sugar*
*2 tbsp maple syrup*
*175 g/6 oz self-raising flour*

*1.* Preheat the oven to 180°C/350°F/Gas Mark 4. Lightly grease two large baking sheets. Roughly chop the nuts.

*2.* Put the butter and sugar into a large bowl and beat with a wooden spoon until creamy, then beat in the maple syrup. Sift in the flour and add three quarters of the nuts. Mix to a rough dough.

*3.* Divide the dough into 16 pieces and roll each piece into a ball. Place the balls on the prepared baking sheets, spaced well apart to allow for spreading. Flatten each ball with your fingertips and scatter over the remaining nuts, pressing them lightly into the dough.

*4.* Bake in the preheated oven for 12–14 minutes, or until pale golden. Leave to cool on the baking sheets for 2–3 minutes, then transfer to a wire rack and leave to cool completely.

# SWEETCORN, COCONUT & LIME COOKIES

**MAKES:** *18–20* | **PREP:** *15–20 mins* | **COOK:** *15–18 mins*

**INGREDIENTS**

*240 g/8½ oz plain flour*
*150 g/5½ oz quick-cook polenta*
*2 tsp baking powder*
*½ tsp bicarbonate of soda*
*½ tsp salt*
*100 g/3½ oz cold coconut oil*
*125 g/4½ oz unsalted butter*
*150 g/5½ oz golden granulated sugar*
*1 egg, lightly beaten*
*175 g/6 oz frozen sweetcorn kernels, thawed and drained*
*2 tbsp finely grated lime rind*

**LIME GLAZE**

*180 g/6¼ oz icing sugar, sifted*
*1 tbsp finely grated lime rind*
*3 tbsp freshly squeezed lime juice*

*1.* Preheat the oven to 180°C/350°F/Gas Mark 4. Line a large baking tray with a silicone sheet.

*2.* Sift together the flour, polenta, baking powder, bicarbonate of soda and salt into a large bowl.

*3.* Put the oil, butter and sugar into a separate large bowl and beat with a hand-held electric mixer for 3–5 minutes until light and fluffy. Gradually beat in the flour mixture and the egg.

*4.* Purée the sweetcorn in a blender until smooth, then add to the mixture with the lime rind.

*5.* Spoon heaped tablespoons of the mixture on the prepared tray, spaced 10 cm/4 inches apart. Lightly flatten the heaps with the back of a spoon.

*6.* Bake in the preheated oven for 15–18 minutes, turning the tray halfway through the cooking time, until the edges are just beginning to brown.

*7.* Carefully transfer to a wire rack and leave to cool completely.

*8.* To make the glaze, combine all the ingredients in a bowl and spoon a little over the top of each cookie.

# GLUTEN-FREE CHOCOLATE BROWNIE COOKIES

**MAKES:** *26* | **PREP:** *30 mins* | **COOK:** *12–14 mins*

**INGREDIENTS**

*55 g/2 oz coconut oil*
*100 g/3½ oz plain chocolate, 70% cocoa solids, broken into pieces*
*55 g/2 oz quinoa flour*
*1 tbsp cocoa powder*
*1 tsp bicarbonate of soda*
*½ tsp ground cinnamon*
*2 eggs*
*150 g/5½ oz light muscovado sugar*
*1 tsp natural vanilla extract*

*1.* Preheat the oven to 190°C/375°F/Gas Mark 5. Line three baking sheets with non-stick baking paper.

*2.* Place the oil and chocolate in a bowl and set over a saucepan of gently simmering water, making sure that the bowl is not touching the water. Heat for 5 minutes, or until the chocolate has melted, then stir to mix.

*3.* Add the quinoa flour, cocoa powder, bicarbonate of soda and cinnamon to a separate bowl and stir together.

*4.* Add the eggs, sugar and vanilla extract to a large mixing bowl and whisk together until thick and frothy. Gently fold in the oil and chocolate mixture, then add the flour mixture and stir until smooth.

*5.* Drop dessertspoons of the brownie mixture onto the prepared trays, spaced well apart to allow for spreading, then bake in the preheated oven for 7–9 minutes until crusty and cracked and still slightly soft to the touch. Leave to cool and harden slightly on the trays, then lift them off the paper and pack into an airtight tin. Eat within 3 days.

3

4

5

# RED VELVET SNOWFLAKE COOKIES

**MAKES:** *55* | **PREP:** *45 mins, plus cooling & setting* | **COOK:** *20–25 mins*

**INGREDIENTS**

*225 g/8 oz butter, at room temperature, diced*
*200 g/7 oz caster sugar*
*1 egg, beaten*
*1 tbsp red food colouring*
*1 tsp vanilla extract*
*1 tsp almond extract*
*350 g/12 oz plain flour, plus extra, for dusting*
*pinch of salt*

**ICING**

*175 g/6 oz icing sugar*
*5 tsp milk*

*1.* Preheat the oven to 180°C/350°F/Gas Mark 4. Line two baking sheets with silicone sheets or greaseproof paper, then set aside.

*2.* Beat the butter and sugar together in a large mixing bowl until creamy. Beat in the egg, food colouring, vanilla extract and almond extract until the colour is evenly distributed.

*3.* Sift the flour and salt into the bowl and beat until combined. Use your hands to mix the dough into a soft ball. Cut the ball into two equal pieces. Roll out one piece of the dough at a time, using a lightly floured roller on a floured surface, to a thickness of 3 mm/⅛ inch. Use a lightly floured 7.5-cm/3-inch snowflake-shaped cutter to stamp out as many cookies as you can, re-rolling the trimmings. Repeat with the remaining dough to make a total of 55 cookies.

*4.* Place the cookies on the prepared baking sheets and bake in the preheated oven for 10–14 minutes until the edges start to brown. Transfer to wire racks and leave to cool completely.

*5.* Meanwhile, make the icing. Sift the icing sugar into a bowl and make a well in the centre. Add the milk to the well, stirring in the sugar from the side to prevent lumps forming. Slowly add more milk, ¼ teaspoon at a time, until the icing is smooth and has a piping consistency. If not using immediately, press a sheet of clingfilm over the surface of the icing to prevent a skin forming.

*6.* Spoon the icing into a piping bag fitted with a small plain nozzle and carefully pipe pretty decorations onto the cookies. Leave to set for 1 hour, then store in an airtight container, layered with greaseproof paper, for up to 3 days.

2
3
4

# PEANUT BUTTER BISCUITS

**MAKES:** *26* | **PREP:** *15 mins* | **COOK:** *12 mins*

**INGREDIENTS**

*115 g/4 oz butter, softened, plus extra for greasing*
*115 g/4 oz crunchy peanut butter*
*115 g/4 oz golden caster sugar*
*115 g/4 oz light muscovado sugar*
*1 egg, beaten*
*½ tsp vanilla extract*
*85 g/3 oz plain flour*
*½ tsp bicarbonate of soda*
*½ tsp baking powder*
*pinch of salt*
*115 g/4 oz rolled oats*

*1.* Preheat the oven to 180°C/350°F/Gas Mark 4, and grease three baking sheets.

*2.* Place the butter and peanut butter in a bowl and beat together. Beat in the caster sugar and muscovado sugar, then gradually beat in the egg and the vanilla extract.

*3.* Sift the flour, bicarbonate of soda, baking powder and salt into the mixture, add the oats and stir until just combined.

*4.* Place spoonfuls of the mixture on the prepared baking sheets, spaced well apart to allow for spreading. Flatten slightly with a fork.

*5.* Bake in the preheated oven for 12 minutes, or until lightly browned. Leave to cool on the baking sheets for 2 minutes, then transfer to wire racks and leave to cool completely.

# MINI FLORENTINES

**MAKES:** *20–30* | **PREP:** *20–25 mins, plus cooling & setting* | **COOK:** *30–35 mins*

**INGREDIENTS**

*75 g/2¾ oz butter*
*75 g/2¾ oz caster sugar*
*25 g/1 oz sultanas or raisins*
*25 g/1 oz glacé cherries, chopped*
*25 g/1 oz crystallized stem ginger, finely chopped*
*25 g/1 oz sunflower seeds*
*100 g/3½ oz flaked almonds*
*2 tbsp double cream*
*175 g/6 oz milk chocolate or plain chocolate, broken into pieces*

*1.* Preheat the oven to 180°C/350°F/ Gas Mark 4. Line two baking trays with baking paper.

*2.* Place the butter in a small saucepan and melt over a low heat. Ad the sugar, stir until dissolved, then bring to the boil.

*3.* Remove from the heat and stir in the sultanas, glacé cherries, crystallized ginger, sunflower seeds and almonds. Mix well, then bea in the cream.

*4.* Place well-spaced teaspoons of the mixture on the prepared baking trays. Bake in the preheated oven for 10–12 minutes, or until light golden in colour.

*5.* Remove from the oven and, while still hot, use a round biscuit cutter to pull in the edges to form perfect rounds. Leave to cool and turn crisp before removing from the trays.

*6.* Put the chocolate into a heatproof bowl set over a saucepan of gently simmering water and heat until melted. Spread most of the chocolate onto a sheet of baking paper. When the chocolate is on th point of setting, place the biscuits flat-side down on the chocolate and leave to harden completely.

*7.* Cut around the florentines and remove from the baking paper. Spread the remaining chocolate on the coated side of the florentine using a fork to mark waves. Leave to set.

# CLASSIC OATMEAL BISCUITS

**MAKES:** *10–20* | **PREP:** *15 mins* | **COOK:** *15 mins*

**NGREDIENTS**

*75 g/6 oz unsalted butter, plus extra for greasing*
*75 g/9¾ oz demerara sugar*
*egg*
*tbsp cold water*
*tsp vanilla extract*
*75 g/13 oz rolled oats*
*40 g/5 oz plain flour, sifted*
*tsp salt*
*tsp bicarbonate of soda*

*1.* Preheat the oven to 180°C/350°F/Gas Mark 4 and grease a large baking sheet.

*2.* Cream the butter and sugar together in a large mixing bowl. Beat in the egg, water and vanilla extract until the mixture is smooth.

*3.* In a separate bowl, mix the oats, flour, salt and bicarbonate of soda together. Gradually stir the oat mixture into the creamed mixture until thoroughly combined.

*4.* Place well-spaced tablespoons of the mixture on the prepared baking sheet. Bake in the preheated oven for 15 minutes, or until golden brown. Remove from the oven , transfer to a wire rack and leave to cool.

*5.* Serve warm or cold.

# GLUTEN-FREE PISTACHIO BISCUITS

**MAKES:** *24* | **PREP:** *25 mins, plus cooling* | **COOK:** *20 mins*

**NGREDIENTS**

*5 g/2 oz skinned pistachio nuts, plus extra to decorate*
*0 g/1½ oz icing sugar*
*tbsp rice flour*
*egg whites*
*5 g/2 oz caster sugar*
*5 g/2 oz desiccated coconut*
*tbsp chopped fresh mint*

*1.* Preheat the oven to 180°C/350°F/Gas Mark 4. Line two baking trays with baking paper.

*2.* Place the pistachio nuts, icing sugar and rice flour in a food processor and process until finely ground.

*3.* Whisk the egg whites in a clean, grease-free bowl until they hold stiff peaks, then gradually whisk in the caster sugar. Fold in the pistachio mixture, coconut and mint.

*4.* Place teaspoons of the mixture on the prepared trays and press a pistachio on top of each to decorate.

*5.* Bake in the preheated oven for about 20 minutes until firm and just beginning to brown. Leave to cool on the tray, then serve.

# CHAI TEA BISCUITS

**MAKES:** *30* | **PREP:** *15–20 mins, plus chilling* | **COOK:** *18–20 mins*

**NGREDIENTS**

*'00 g/3½ oz soft light brown sugar*
*? tbsp dry chai tea (about 4 teabags)*
*4 tsp salt*
*'25 g/4½ oz wholemeal flour, plus extra for dusting*
*tsp vanilla extract*
*15 g/4 oz cold unsalted butter*

*1.* Preheat the oven to 180°C/350°F/Gas Mark 4 and line a baking tray with baking paper.

*2.* Put the sugar, tea and salt into a food processor and whizz until the tea has been ground to a fine powder. Add the flour, vanilla extract and butter and process until well combined and the mixture begins to hold together. If the mixture is too dry, add cold water, ½ teaspoon at a time, and whizz until the mixture just comes together. Turn out the dough onto a sheet of clingfilm and shape into a log. Wrap tightly and chill in the refrigerator for 15 minutes.

*3.* Roll out the dough on a lightly floured surface to about 3 mm/⅛ inch thick and cut into rounds with a 6-cm/2½-inch round biscuit cutter (or use the shape of your choice). Transfer the biscuits to the prepared tray and bake in the preheated oven for 18–20 minutes, or until they begin to colour.

*4.* Remove from the oven, transfer to a wire rack and leave to cool completely. Serve at room temperature.

2
3
4

# SHORTBREAD

**MAKES:** *8 pieces* | **PREP:** *15 mins* | **COOK:** *15–20 mins*

**NGREDIENTS**

*25 g/4½ oz lightly salted butter, softened, plus extra for greasing*

*5 g/2 oz caster sugar, plus extra for sprinkling*

*50 g/5½ oz plain flour*

*5 g/1 oz cornflour*

*1.* Preheat the oven to 190°C/375°F/Gas Mark 5. Lightly grease a baking sheet and a 20-cm/8-inch metal flan ring. Place the ring on the prepared baking sheet.

*2.* Put the butter and sugar into a large bowl and beat with a wooden spoon until very creamy. Sift in the flour and cornflour and mix until fine crumbs form.

*3.* Gather the mixture together with your hands and gently knead to a smooth dough. Press the dough into the ring and, using your knuckles, spread to the edge. Level the surface with a small angled palette knife. Prick the dough all over with a fork and mark into eight triangles with a knife.

*4.* Bake in the preheated oven for 15–20 minutes, or until golden around the edge. Carefully cut the hot shortbread into triangles along the knife marks and sprinkle with sugar. Gently remove the ring and leave the shortbread to cool on the baking sheet.

# SNICKERDOODLES

**MAKES:** *40* | **PREP:** *15 mins, plus chilling* | **COOK:** *10–12 mins*

**INGREDIENTS**

*225 g/8 oz butter, softened*
*140 g/5 oz caster sugar*
*2 large eggs, lightly beaten*
*1 tsp vanilla extract*
*400 g/14 oz plain flour*
*1 tsp bicarbonate of soda*
*½ tsp freshly grated nutmeg*
*pinch of salt*
*55 g/2 oz pecan nuts, finely chopped*

**CINNAMON COATING**

*1 tbsp caster sugar*
*2 tbsp ground cinnamon*

*1.* Put the butter and sugar into a bowl and mix well with a wooden spoon, then beat in the eggs and vanilla extract. Sift together the flour, bicarbonate of soda, nutmeg and a pinch of salt into the mixture, add the pecan nuts and stir until thoroughly combined.

*2.* Shape the dough into a ball, wrap in clingfilm and chill in the refrigerator for 30–60 minutes.

*3.* Preheat the oven to 190°C/375°F/Gas Mark 5. Line two or three baking sheets with greaseproof paper.

*4.* To make the cinnamon coating, mix the caster sugar and cinnamon together in a shallow dish. Scoop up tablespoons of the cookie dough and roll into balls. Roll each ball in the cinnamon mixture to coat and place on the prepared baking sheets, spaced well apart to allow for spreading.

*5.* Bake in the preheated oven for 10–12 minutes until golden brown. Leave to cool on the baking sheets for 5–10 minutes, then, using a palette knife, transfer to wire racks and leave to cool completely.

1
2
4

# GINGERSNAPS

**MAKES:** *30* | **PREP:** *20 mins* | **COOK:** *25–30 mins*

**NGREDIENTS**

*25 g/4½ oz butter, plus extra for greasing*
*50 g/12 oz self-raising flour*
*inch of salt*
*00 g/7 oz caster sugar*
*tbsp ground ginger*
*tsp bicarbonate of soda*
*5 g/2¾ oz golden syrup*
*egg, beaten*
*tsp grated orange rind*

*1.* Preheat the oven to 160°C/325°F/Gas Mark 3. Lightly grease two baking sheets.

*2.* Sift together the flour, salt, sugar, ginger and bicarbonate of soda into a large mixing bowl.

*3.* Heat the butter and golden syrup together in a saucepan over a very low heat until the butter has melted. Remove from the heat and leave to cool slightly, then pour the contents onto the dry ingredients.

*4.* Add the egg and orange rind and mix thoroughly until a dough forms. Using your hands, carefully shape into 30 even-sized balls.

*5.* Put the balls on the prepared baking sheets, , spaced well apart to allow for spreading, then flatten them slightly with your fingertips.

*6.* Bake in the preheated oven for 15–20 minutes, then carefully transfer to a wire rack and leave to cool.

# VEGAN MOCHA BISCUITS

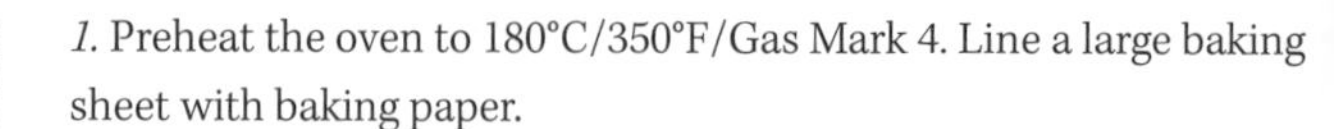

**MAKES:** *14* | **PREP:** *10–15 mins* | **COOK:** *15 mins*

**INGREDIENTS**

*115 g/4 oz plain flour*
*¼ tsp baking powder*
*15 g/½ oz cocoa powder*
*125 g/4½ oz brown sugar*
*1 tbsp espresso powder*
*1 tbsp boiling water*
*125 g/4½ oz vegan margarine*
*50 g/1¾ oz porridge oats*

*1.* Preheat the oven to 180°C/350°F/Gas Mark 4. Line a large baking sheet with baking paper.

*2.* Sift together the flour, baking powder and cocoa powder into a large mixing bowl. Add the sugar and mix to combine.

*3.* Dissolve the espresso powder in the water and stir into the bowl. Add the margarine and oats and mix to a soft dough.

*4.* Shape the mixture into 14 small balls, place on the prepared baking sheet, spaced well apart to allow for spreading, and flatten slightly. Bake in the preheated oven for 15 minutes, or until crisp. Transfer to a wire rack and leave to cool completely before serving o storing in an airtight jar for up to 5 days.

# LEMON CHOCOLATE PINWHEELS

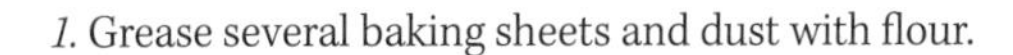

**MAKES:** *40* | **PREP:** *20 mins, plus chilling* | **COOK:** *20–22 mins*

**IGREDIENTS**

*75 g/6 oz butter, softened, plus extra for greasing*
*50 g/9 oz caster sugar*
*egg, beaten*
*50 g/12 oz plain flour, plus extra for dusting*
*5 g/1 oz plain chocolate, broken into pieces*
*ated rind of 1 lemon*

*1.* Grease several baking sheets and dust with flour.

*2.* In a large mixing bowl, cream together the butter and sugar until pale and fluffy. Gradually add the egg to the mixture, beating well after each addition.

*3.* Sift in the flour and mix to a soft dough. Transfer half the dough to a separate bowl.

*4.* Put the chocolate into a heatproof bowl set over a saucepan of gently simmering water and heat until melted. Leave to cool slightly, then beat it into one half of the dough.

*5.* Stir the lemon rind into the other half of the dough. On a lightly floured work surface, roll out the each dough to a rectangle with a thickness of 1 cm/½ inch.

*6.* Lay the lemon dough on top of the chocolate dough. Roll up tightly, using a sheet of baking paper to guide you. Chill in the refrigerator for 1 hour.

*7.* Preheat the oven to 190°C/375°F/Gas Mark 5. Cut the roll into 40 slices, place on the prepared baking sheets and bake in the preheated oven for 10–12 minutes, or until lightly golden. Transfer to a wire rack and leave to cool completely before serving.

# CHOCOLATE-DIPPED CHERRY & PISTACHIO BISCOTTI

**MAKES:** *40* | **PREP:** *25 mins* | **COOK:** *40–45 mins*

**INGREDIENTS**

*2 sprays non-stick cooking spray*
*250 g/9 oz plain flour, plus extra for dusting*
*125 g/4½ oz wholemeal flour*
*¼ tsp salt*
*200 g/7 oz granulated sugar*
*3 eggs*
*2 tbsp vegetable oil*
*1 tbsp vanilla extract*
*40 g/1½ oz dried cherries, roughly chopped*
*60 g/2¼ oz roasted, unsalted pistachio nuts*
*280 g/10 oz plain chocolate, chopped*

*1.* Preheat the oven to 180°C/350°F/Gas Mark 4 and line a large baking sheet with baking paper. Spray the paper with cooking spray

*2.* Put the plain flour, wholemeal flour and salt into a mixing bowl.

*3.* Put the sugar and eggs into a separate bowl and beat with a hand-held electric mixer on high speed for 3–4 minutes, or until the mixture is thick and pale yellow. Add the oil and vanilla extract and beat to incorporate. Add the dry mixture to the wet mixture and beat on low speed until just combined. Add the cherries and nuts and mix to incorporate.

*4.* Divide the dough into two pieces and turn them out onto the prepared baking sheet. With floured hands, shape each piece of dough into a 25-cm/10-inch loaf and flatten it to 2.5 cm/1 inch, squaring off the edges with your hands. Bake in the preheated oven for 25 minutes, or until light brown. Remove from the oven and leav to cool on the baking sheet for about 10 minutes. Meanwhile, reduc the oven temperature to 160°C/325°F/Gas Mark 3.

*5.* Slice each loaf into twenty 1-cm/½-inch thick slices. Arrange cut-side down on the baking sheet and return to the oven for a further 10 minutes. Flip and bake for a further 10 minutes. Remove from th oven, transfer to a wire rack and leave to cool completely.

*6.* Put the chocolate into a heatproof bowl set over a saucepan of gently simmering water and heat until melted. Dip one flat side of each of the biscotti into the chocolate, then return to the baking sheet, setting down on the uncoated side, and leave to cool for 10–1 minutes until the chocolate is set. Serve at room temperature.

2
3
5

# RASPBERRY & PINK PEPPERCORN MACAROONS

**MAKES:** *20* | **PREP:** *15–20 mins, plus standing* | **COOK:** *15 mins*

**NGREDIENTS**

*75 g/6 oz icing sugar*
*25 g/4½ oz ground almonds*
*egg whites*
*0 g/2½ oz caster sugar*
*–2 tsp natural pink food colouring*

**ILLING**

*50 g/5½ oz butter, softened*
*0 g/2½ oz icing sugar*
*–2 tbsp raspberry jam*
*tsp crushed pink peppercorns*

*1.* Preheat the oven to 140°C/275°F/Gas Mark 1. Line two baking trays with baking paper.

*2.* Place the icing sugar and ground almonds in a blender and blend until very fine and evenly ground. Sift into a bowl.

*3.* Place the egg whites in a mixing bowl and whisk with a hand-held electric mixer until they hold soft peaks. Gradually add the sugar, a teaspoon at a time, until the mixture is smooth and glossy. Beat in the food colouring until evenly distributed.

*4.* Fold the ground almond and sugar mixture into the egg whites, one third at a time, until well combined. Spoon into a piping bag fitted with a 1-cm/½-inch plain nozzle.

*5.* Pipe 40 small rounds, about 3 cm/1¼ inches in diameter, onto the prepared trays. Sharply tap the trays on the work surface and leave to stand at room temperature for 15–20 minutes until a skin forms on the rounds. Bake in the preheated oven for 15 minutes, then leave to cool on the trays.

*6.* To make the filling, beat together the butter and icing sugar until smooth. Beat in the raspberry jam and the peppercorns. Spoon into a piping bag fitted with a plain nozzle, pipe a little into the macaroons, sandwich together and serve immediately.

CHAPTER FOUR

# SWEET PIES & PASTRIES

# VEGAN ZESTY LIME PIE

**SERVES:** *8* | **PREP:** *25 mins, plus cooling & chilling* | **COOK:** *12–15 mins*

**NGREDIENTS**

**ASE**

*00 g/3½ oz coconut oil*
*70 g/9½ oz wholemeal plain flour, plus extra for dusting*
*tbsp cold water*

**ILLING**

*70 g/1 lb firm tofu*
*0 ml/2 fl oz lime juice*
*75 g/6 oz brown sugar*
*tbsp cornflour*
*tsp lime zest*

*1.* Preheat the oven to 200°C/400°F/Gas Mark 6.

*2.* To make the base, rub the coconut oil into the flour and gradually add the water to bring the dough together. This can be done by hand or using a food processor.

*3.* Roll out the dough on a lightly floured surface and use to line a 25-cm/10-inch loose-based tart tin. Bake in the preheated oven for 12–15 minutes until golden and crisp. Leave to cool.

*4.* Place all the ingredients for the filling except the lime zest in the bowl of a food processor and process for 1–2 minutes until smooth. Stir in the lime zest.

*5.* Spoon the tart filling into the pastry case, smoothing it with a rubber spatula. Transfer to the refrigerator and chill for at least 1 hour before serving.

1
3
5

# LEMON MERINGUE PIE

**SERVES:** *6–8* | **PREP:** *20 mins, plus chilling* | **COOK:** *1 hour 5 mins*

**NGREDIENTS**

*50 g/5½ oz plain flour, plus extra for dusting*
*5 g/3 oz butter, cut into small pieces, plus extra for greasing*
*5 g/1¼ oz icing sugar, sifted*
*inely grated rind of 1 lemon*
*2 egg yolk, beaten*
*½ tbsp milk*

**ILLING**

*tbsp cornflour*
*00 ml /10 fl oz cold water*
*uice of 2 lemons*
*75 g/6 oz caster sugar*
*eggs, separated*

*1.* Sift the flour into a bowl. Rub in the butter with your fingertips until the mixture resembles fine breadcrumbs. Mix in the icing sugar, lemon rind, egg yolk and milk.

*2.* Turn out the pastry onto a lightly floured surface and briefly knead. Wrap in clingfilm and chill in the refrigerator for 30 minutes.

*3.* Preheat the oven to 180°C/350°F/Gas Mark 4. Grease a 20-cm/8-inch round tart tin. Roll out the pastry to a thickness of 5 mm/¼ inch, then use it to line the tin. Prick all over with a fork, line with baking paper and fill with baking beans. Bake in the preheated oven for 15 minutes.

*4.* Remove the pastry case from the oven and take out the paper and beans. Reduce the oven temperature to 150°C/300°F/Gas Mark 2.

*5.* To make the filling, mix the cornflour with a little of the water to make a paste. Put the remaining water in a saucepan. Stir the lemon juice and rind into the cornflour paste. Bring to the boil, stirring. Reduce the heat and cook for 2 minutes, then remove from the heat and leave to cool slightly. Stir in 5 tablespoons of the sugar and the egg yolks, and pour into the pastry case.

*6.* Whisk the egg whites in a clean, grease-free bowl until they hold stiff peaks. Gradually whisk in the remaining sugar and spread over the pie. Place on a baking sheet and bake for 40 minutes. Remove from the oven and leave to cool, then cut into wedges and serve.

# APPLE PIE

**SERVES:** *6* | **PREP:** *45 mins, plus chilling* | **COOK:** *50 mins*

**INGREDIENTS**

**PASTRY**

*350 g/12 oz plain flour, plus extra for dusting*
*pinch of salt*
*85 g/3 oz butter or margarine, diced*
*85 g/3 oz lard or white vegetable fat, diced*
*6 tbsp cold water*
*beaten egg or milk, for glazing*

**FILLING**

*750 g–1 kg/1 lb 10 oz–2 lb 4 oz cooking apples, peeled, cored and sliced*
*125 g/4½ oz caster sugar, plus extra for sprinkling*
*½–1 tsp ground cinnamon, mixed spice or ground ginger*

*1.* To make the pastry, sift the flour and salt into a mixing bowl. Add the butter and lard and rub in with your fingertips until the mixture resembles fine breadcrumbs. Add the water and gather the mixture together into a dough. Wrap the dough in clingfilm and chill in the refrigerator for 30 minutes. Preheat the oven to 220°C/425°F/Gas Mark 7. Thinly roll out almost two thirds of the pastry on a lightly floured surface and use to line a 23-cm/9-inch deep pie dish.

*2.* To make the filling, place the apple slices, sugar and spice in a bowl and mix thoroughly together. Pack the apple mixture into the pastry case; the filling can come up above the rim. Add 1–2 tablespoons of water if needed.

*3.* Roll out the remaining pastry on a lightly floured surface to make a lid. Dampen the edges of the pie rim with water and position the lid, pressing the edges firmly together. Trim and crimp the edges. Use the trimmings to cut out decorations. Dampen and attach.

*4.* Glaze the top of the pie with beaten egg, make 1–2 slits in the top and place the pie dish on a baking sheet. Bake in the preheated oven for 20 minutes, then reduce the oven temperature to 180°C/350°F/Gas Mark 4 and bake for a further 30 minutes, or until the pastry is golden brown. Serve hot or cold.

# TARTE TATIN

**SERVES:** *6* | **PREP:** *25 mins* | **COOK:** *35–40 mins, plus resting*

**NGREDIENTS**

*00 g/7 oz caster sugar*
*50 g/5½ oz unsalted butter*
*00 g/1 lb 12 oz Cox or Golden Delicious apples*
*lain flour, for dusting*
*50 g/12 oz puff pastry*
*anilla ice cream, to serve*

*1.* Place a 20-cm/8-inch ovenproof frying pan over a low heat and add the sugar. Heat the sugar until it starts to caramelize, but do not allow it to burn, then add the butter and stir it in to make a light toffee sauce. Remove from the heat.

*2.* Peel the apples and cut them into eighths vertically. Core the apples and lay them in the pan on top of the toffee sauce, cut side up. They should fill the pan. If there are any large gaps, add a few more apple pieces. Place the pan over a medium heat and cover. Simmer, without stirring, for about 5–10 minutes until the apples have soaked up some of the sauce, then remove from the heat.

*3.* Preheat the oven to 190°C/375°F/Gas Mark 5. Roll out the pastry on a floured surface so that it will thickly cover the pan, with extra overhanging the side of the pan. Lay the pastry on top of the apples and tuck the edges down inside between the fruit and the pan until it is sealed. Don't worry about making it look too neat – it will be turned over before serving.

*4.* Bake in the preheated oven for 25–35 minutes, checking to make sure the pastry doesn't burn. The pastry should be puffed and golden. Remove from the oven and leave to rest for 30–60 minutes.

*5.* To serve, place a plate on top of the pan while the tart is still a little warm. Carefully turn it over and lift off the pan. Cut into wedges and serve with vanilla ice cream.

# HALLOWEEN MUD PIE

**SERVES:** *6–8* | **PREP:** *30 mins* | **COOK:** *35–40 mins*

**NGREDIENTS**

*5 g/3 oz plain chocolate*
*5 g/3 oz unsalted butter*
*5 g/3 oz light muscovado sugar*
*eggs, beaten*
*00 ml/3½ fl oz single cream*
*tsp vanilla extract*

**ASTRY**

*75 g/6 oz plain flour, plus extra for dusting*
*5 g/1 oz cocoa powder*
*0 g/1½ oz light muscovado sugar*
*5 g/3 oz unsalted butter*
*–3 tbsp cold water*

**OPPING**

*50 ml/9 fl oz whipping cream*
*5 g/3 oz plain chocolate*

*1.* Preheat the oven to 200°C/400°F/Gas Mark 6. To make the pastry, sift the flour and cocoa powder into a bowl and stir in the sugar. Rub in the butter with your fingertips until the mixture resembles fine breadcrumbs. Add just enough water to bind to a dough.

*2.* Roll out the dough on a lightly floured work surface to a round large enough to line a 20-cm/8-inch, 3-cm/1¼-inch deep flan tin. Use the pastry to line the tin. Prick the base with a fork, cover with a piece of greaseproof paper and fill with baking beans, then blind-bake in the preheated oven for 10 minutes. Remove from the oven and take out the greaseproof paper and beans. Reduce the oven temperature to 180°C/350°F/Gas Mark 4.

*3.* Put the chocolate and butter into a saucepan and heat over a low heat, stirring, until melted. Put the sugar and eggs into a bowl and whisk together until smooth, then stir in the chocolate mixture, cream and vanilla extract.

*4.* Pour the chocolate mixture into the pastry case and bake in the oven for 20–25 minutes, or until just set. Leave to cool.

*5.* To make the topping, whip the cream until it just holds its shape, then spread over the pie. Put the chocolate into a bowl set over a saucepan of gently simmering water and heat until melted, then spoon into a piping bag and pipe decorations over the cream. Serve the pie cold.

# PUMPKIN PIE

**SERVES:** *8* | **PREP:** *25 mins, plus cooling & chilling* | **COOK:** *50 mins–1 hour*

**INGREDIENTS**

*plain flour, for dusting*
*350 g/12 oz ready-made shortcrust pastry*
*400 g/14 oz pumpkin purée*
*2 eggs, lightly beaten*
*150 g/5½ oz white sugar*
*1 tsp ground cinnamon*
*½ tsp ground ginger*
*¼ tsp ground cloves*
*½ tsp salt*
*350 ml/12 fl oz canned evaporated milk*

**EGGNOG WHIPPED CREAM**

*350 ml/12 fl oz double cream*
*70 g/2½ oz icing sugar*
*1 tbsp brandy, or to taste*
*1 tbsp light or dark rum, or to taste*
*freshly grated nutmeg, to decorate*

*1.* Preheat the oven to 200°C/400°F/Gas Mark 6. Very lightly dust a rolling pin with flour and use to roll out the pastry on a lightly floured surface into a 30-cm/12-inch round. Line a 23-cm/9-inch deep pie dish with the pastry, trimming the excess. Line the pastry case with baking paper and fill with baking beans. Bake in the preheated oven for 10 minutes, then remove from the oven and take out the paper and beans. Reduce the oven temperature to 180°C/350°F/Gas Mark 4.

*2.* Meanwhile, put the pumpkin purée, eggs, sugar, cinnamon, ginger, cloves and salt into a bowl and beat together, then beat in the evaporated milk. Pour the mixture into the pastry case, return to the oven, and bake for 40–50 minutes until the filling is set and a knife inserted into the centre comes out clean. Transfer to a wire rack and leave to cool.

*3.* While the pie is baking, make the eggnog whipped cream. Put the cream in a bowl and beat until it has thickened and increased in volume. Just as it starts to stiffen, sift in the icing sugar and continue beating until it holds stiff peaks. Add the brandy and rum and beat, taking care not to overbeat or the mixture will separate. Cover and chill until required. Grate some nutmeg over the whipped cream and serve with the pie.

1

2

3

# BANOFFEE PIE

**SERVES:** *6–8* | **PREP:** *30 mins, plus cooling* | **COOK:** *2 hours 20 mins–2 hours 25 mins*

**NGREDIENTS**

**ILLING**

*cans sweetened condensed milk, weighing 400 g/14 oz each*

*ripe bananas*

*uice of ½ lemon*

*tsp vanilla extract*

*5 g/2¾ oz plain chocolate, grated*

*75 ml/16 fl oz double cream, whipped*

**ISCUIT BASE**

*5 g/3 oz butter, melted, plus extra for greasing*

*50 g/5½ oz digestive biscuits, crushed*

*5 g/1 oz almonds, toasted and ground*

*5 g/1 oz hazelnuts, toasted and ground*

*1.* To make the filling, place the unopened cans of milk in a large saucepan and add enough water to cover them. Bring to the boil, then reduce the heat and simmer for 2 hours, topping up the water level to keep the cans covered. Carefully lift out the hot cans from the pan and leave to cool.

*2.* Preheat the oven to 180°C/350°F/Gas Mark 4 and grease a 23-cm/9-inch tart tin. To make the biscuit base, put the butter into a bowl and add the biscuits and nuts. Mix well together, then press the mixture evenly into the base and sides of the prepared tin. Bake in the preheated oven for 10–12 minutes. Leave to cool.

*3.* Peel and slice the bananas and place in a bowl. Add the lemon juice and vanilla extract and mix together. Spread the banana mixture over the biscuit base, then spoon in the contents of the cooled cans of condensed milk.

*4.* Sprinkle over 50 g/1¾ oz of the chocolate, then top with a layer of whipped cream. Sprinkle over the remaining chocolate and serve the pie at room temperature.

# NEW YORK CHEESECAKE

**SERVES:** *10* | **PREP:** *40 mins, plus cooling & chilling* | **COOK:** *55 mins*

**INGREDIENTS**

*100 g/3½ oz butter, plus extra for greasing*
*150 g/5½ oz digestive biscuits, finely crushed*
*1 tbsp granulated sugar*
*900 g/2 lb cream cheese*
*250 g/9 oz caster sugar*
*2 tbsp plain flour*
*1 tsp vanilla extract*
*finely grated zest of 1 orange*
*finely grated zest of 1 lemon*
*3 eggs*
*2 egg yolks*
*300 ml/10 fl oz double cream*

*1.* Preheat the oven to 180°C/350°F/Gas Mark 4. Melt the butter in a small saucepan. Remove from the heat and stir in the biscuits and granulated sugar.

*2.* Press the biscuit mixture tightly into the base of a 23-cm/9-inch round springform cake tin. Bake in the preheated oven for 10 minutes. Remove from the oven, place the tin on a wire rack. and leave to cool completely

*3.* Increase the oven temperature to 200°C/400°F/Gas Mark 6. Use a hand-held electric mixer to beat the cheese until creamy, then gradually add the caster sugar and flour and beat until smooth. Increase the speed and beat in the vanilla extract, orange zest and lemon zest, then beat in the eggs and egg yolks, one at a time. Finall beat in the cream. Scrape any excess from the sides and paddles of the beater into the mixture. It should be light and fluffy – beat on a faster setting if you need to.

*4.* Grease the side of the cake tin and pour in the filling. Smooth the top and bake for 15 minutes, then reduce the oven temperature to 110°C/225°F/Gas Mark ¼ and bake for a further 30 minutes. Switch off the oven and leave the cheesecake inside for 2 hours to cool and set. Chill in the refrigerator overnight before serving.

*5.* Slide a knife around the edge of the cake, then release the springform and remove the cake from the tin to serve.

1
2
4

# BLOOD ORANGE POLENTA TART

**SERVES:** *8* | **PREP:** *15–20 mins* | **COOK:** *40–45 mins, plus cooling*

**INGREDIENTS**

*about 4 sprays of cooking spray*
*250 g/9 oz cooked polenta*
*55 g/2 oz soft light brown sugar, plus extra for sprinkling*
*3 blood oranges or small navel oranges*

**FILLING**

*4 eggs*
*40 g/5 oz caster sugar*
*50 ml/5 fl oz orange juice*
*tbsp lemon juice*
*25 ml/4 fl oz semi-skimmed milk*
*½ tsp vanilla extract*
*tsp finely grated orange rind*

*1.* Preheat the oven to 180°C/350°F/Gas Mark 4. Spray a 23-cm/9-inch springform tart tin with cooking spray.

*2.* To make the tart case, put the polenta and brown sugar into a medium-sized bowl and mix well. Spread the mixture in the prepared tin in a thin layer and bake in the preheated oven for about 20 minutes, or until it begins to colour.

*3.* To make the filling, whisk together the eggs, sugar, orange juice, lemon juice, milk and vanilla extract. Stir in the orange rind, then pour the mixture into the polenta case in an even layer. Bake in the preheated oven for about 15 minutes, or until the filling begins to set.

*4.* Meanwhile, slice the oranges into thin rounds, using a serrated knife. When the filling is partly set, remove the tart from the oven and arrange the orange slices on top. Sprinkle some brown sugar over the top and return the tart to the oven. Bake for a further 6–8 minutes, or until the filling is almost set.

*5.* Remove from the oven, place the tin on a wire rack and leave to cool. Slice the tart into wedges and serve.

# SUMMER FRUIT TARTLETS

**MAKES:** *12* | **PREP:** *20–25 mins, plus chilling* | **COOK:** *12–18 mins, plus cooling*

**INGREDIENTS**

*200 g/7 oz plain flour, plus extra for dusting*
*85 g/3 oz icing sugar, plus extra for dusting*
*55 g/2 oz ground almonds*
*115 g/4 oz butter*
*1 egg yolk*
*1 tbsp milk*

**FILLING**

*225 g/8 oz cream cheese*
*sifted icing sugar, to taste*
*350 g/12 oz fresh summer berries*

*1.* Sift together the flour and icing sugar into a bowl. Stir in the almonds. Add the butter, rubbing it in with your fingertips until the mixture resembles breadcrumbs. Add the egg yolk and milk and work in until the dough comes together. Wrap in clingfilm and chill in the refrigerator for 30 minutes.

*2.* Preheat the oven to 200°C/400°F/Gas Mark 6. Roll out the dough on a lightly floured surface and use it to line 12 deep tartlet tins. Prick the bases and press a piece of foil into each.

*3.* Bake in the preheated oven for 10–15 minutes, or until light golden brown. Remove the foil and bake for a further 2–3 minutes. Transfer to a wire rack and leave to cool.

*4.* To make the filling, mix the cream cheese and icing sugar together in a bowl. Place a spoonful of filling in each tartlet and arrange the berries on top. Dust with icing sugar and serve immediately.

# MINI CHERRY PIES

**MAKES:** *24* | **PREP:** *25 mins* | **COOK:** *15 mins*

**NGREDIENTS**

*utter, for greasing*
*50 g/12 oz cherries, stoned*
*tsp cornflour*
*tbsp cherry jam*
*rated rind of 2 limes*
*lain flour, for dusting*
*50 g/1 lb ready-made sweet shortcrust pastry, chilled*
*egg yolk mixed with 1 tbsp water, for glazing*
*aster sugar, for sprinkling*

*1.* Preheat the oven to 180°C/350°F/Gas Mark 4. Grease two 12-hole muffin tins.

*2.* Roughly chop the cherries. Put them into a mixing bowl and stir in the cornflour, jam and lime rind.

*3.* Thinly roll out half the pastry on a lightly floured surface. Using a 6-cm/2½-inch round fluted cookie cutter, stamp out 24 rounds. Gently press into the prepared tin, re-rolling the trimmings as needed. Brush the top edges of the pie cases with a little of the egg glaze, then spoon in the filling.

*4.* Thinly roll out the remaining pastry on a lightly floured surface. Use a 5-cm/2-inch round cutter to stamp out 24 rounds, re-rolling the trimmings as needed. Attach the rounds as lids to the base of the pies with water, pressing the edges together. Use a cookie cutter to cut out mini hearts from the pastry and attach them to the lids with water. Brush the egg glaze over the pastry and sprinkle with sugar.

*5.* Bake in the preheated oven for 15 minutes, or until golden. Leave to cool in the tins for 10 minutes, then loosen with a round-bladed knife, transfer to a wire rack and leave to cool completely.

# APRICOT ALMOND TART

**SERVES:** *6–8* | **PREP:** *30 mins* | **COOK:** *50–55 mins*

**NGREDIENTS**

*5 g/3 oz unsalted butter, softened*
*5 g/3 oz caster sugar*
*large egg, beaten*
*40 g/5 oz ground almonds*
*0 g/1½ oz plain flour*
*½ tsp almond extract*
*0–12 apricots, stoned and quartered*
*tbsp apricot jam*
*tbsp water*

**ASTRY**

*75 g/6 oz plain flour, plus extra for dusting*
*00 g/3½ oz cold unsalted butter*
*tbsp icing sugar*
*egg yolk*
*tbsp orange juice*

*1.* Preheat the oven to 190°C/375°F/Gas Mark 5. To make the pastry, put the flour, butter and icing sugar into a food processor and process to fine crumbs. Mix the egg yolk and orange juice together and stir into the flour mixture to make a soft dough.

*2.* Turn out the pastry onto a lightly floured surface and roll out to a round large enough to line a 23-cm/9-inch loose-based flan tin. Prick the base with a fork, cover with a piece of greaseproof paper and fill with baking beans. Blind-bake in the preheated oven for 10 minutes. Remove from the oven and take out the paper and beans.

*3.* Put the butter, sugar, egg, almonds, flour and almond extract into a food processor and process to a smooth paste.

*4.* Spread the almond filling over the base of the pastry case and arrange the apricots cut side up on top. Reduce the oven temperature to 180°C/350°F/Gas Mark 4 and bake the tart for 35–40 minutes until the filling is set and golden brown.

*5.* Put the jam into a small saucepan with the water and gently heat until melted. Brush over the apricots and serve.

# COFFEE TARTS

**MAKES:** *12* | **PREP:** *45 mins, plus standing, chilling & cooling* | **COOK:** *30–35 mins*

**INGREDIENTS**

*butter, for greasing*
*plain flour, for dusting*
*450 g/1 lb ready-made sweet shortcrust pastry, chilled*
*225 ml/8 fl oz semi-skimmed milk*
*115 g/4 oz plain chocolate, roughly chopped*
*2 tsp instant coffee powder or granules*
*2 tbsp caster sugar*
*2 eggs*
*2 egg yolks*

**DECORATION**

*200 ml/7 fl oz double cream*
*2 tbsp icing sugar*
*2 tbsp coffee cream liqueur*
*1½ tsp instant coffee dissolved in 1 tsp boiling water*
*white chocolate curls, to decorate*
*sifted cocoa powder, to decorate*

*1.* Lightly grease a 12-hole muffin tin. Thinly roll out the pastry on a lightly floured surface. Using a 10-cm/4-inch round cutter, stamp ou 12 rounds. Press these gently into the prepared tin. Prick the base of each with a fork, then chill in the refrigerator for 15 minutes. Prehea the oven to 190°C/375°F/Gas Mark 5.

*2.* Line the pastry cases with squares of crumpled baking paper and baking beans. Bake in the preheated oven for 10 minutes, then remove the paper and beans and bake the cases for a further 2–3 minutes, or until the bases are crisp. Reduce the oven temperature t 160°C/325°F/Gas Mark 3. Meanwhile, bring the milk just to the boil in a small saucepan. Remove from the heat, add the chocolate, coffe and caster sugar and leave to stand until the chocolate has melted.

*3.* Beat together the eggs and egg yolks in a mixing bowl, then gradually whisk in the warm milk mixture until smooth. Pour the custard into the pastry cases.

*4.* Bake for 15–20 minutes, or until just set. Leave to cool in the tin fc 10 minutes, then loosen with a round-bladed knife and transfer to a wire rack. Whip the cream in a bowl until it holds soft peaks. Add th sugar, then whisk in the liqueur and coffee until thick. Spoon over the pies, then decorate with white chocolate curls and a dusting of cocoa powder.

# MOUSSE-AU-CHOCOLAT TARTLETS

**MAKES:** *6* | **PREP:** *45 mins, plus chilling & cooling* | **COOK:** *45 mins*

**IGREDIENTS**

**ASTRY**

*50 g/9 oz plain flour, plus extra for dusting*
*inch of salt*
*) g/1¾ oz caster sugar*
*40 g/5 oz butter*
*egg*
*nely grated rind of 1 lemon*

**LLING**

*75 ml/13 fl oz single cream*
*50 g/12 oz plain chocolate, 70% cocoa solids, broken into pieces*
*egg yolks*
*5 g/2 oz caster sugar*
*½ tbsp water*
*a salt flakes, to decorate (optional)*

*1.* Preheat the oven to 180°C/350°F/Gas Mark 4. To make the pastry, put the flour, salt, sugar, butter, egg and lemon rind into a bowl and mix together. Roll the pastry into a ball, wrap in clingfilm and chill in the refrigerator for 30 minutes.

*2.* Roll out the pastry on a lightly floured surface, then use a 10-cm/4-inch round cutter to stamp out six rounds. Use them to line six tartlet tins, then line with baking paper and fill with baking beans. Bake in the preheated oven for 15 minutes, then remove the beans and paper and bake for a further 10 minutes.

*3.* To make the filling, heat the cream in a heatproof bowl set over a saucepan of gently simmering water, then add the chocolate and heat until melted. Remove from the heat and leave to stand until cooled to room temperature.

*4.* Put the egg yolks, sugar and water into a separate heatproof bowl set over a saucepan of gently simmering water and heat, whisking constantly, for 8–10 minutes until the mixture thickens. Remove from the heat, stir into the chocolate mixture and beat with a hand-held electric mixer for 5–6 minutes.

*5.* Pour the filling into the pastry cases. Carefully transfer to the refrigerator and chill for 2–3 hours, or until the filling is firm. Serve chilled, decorated with sea salt flakes, if using.

# DATE, PISTACHIO & HONEY SLICES

**MAKES:** *12* | **PREP:** *30 mins* | **COOK:** *30–35 mins*

**INGREDIENTS**

*250 g/9 oz ready-to-eat dried dates, stoned and chopped*
*2 tbsp lemon juice*
*2 tbsp water*
*85 g/3 oz pistachio nuts, chopped*
*2 tbsp clear honey*
*1 tbsp milk, for glazing*

**PASTRY**

*225 g/8 oz plain flour, plus extra for dusting*
*25 g/1 oz golden caster sugar*
*150 g/5½ oz butter*
*4–5 tbsp cold water*

*1.* Put the dates, lemon juice and water into a saucepan and bring to the boil, stirring. Remove from the heat, stir in the nuts and 1 tablespoon of the honey, then cover and leave to cool.

*2.* Preheat the oven to 200°C/400°F/Gas Mark 6. To make the pastry, put the flour, sugar and butter into a food processor and process to fine crumbs. Mix in just enough cold water to bind to a soft, not sticky, dough.

*3.* Roll out the pastry on a floured surface to two 30 x 20-cm/12 x 8-inch rectangles. Place one rectangle on a baking sheet. Spread the date and nut mixture to within 1 cm/½ inch of the edge. Top with the remaining pastry rectangle.

*4.* Press to seal, trim the edges and mark into 12 slices. Glaze with th milk and bake in the preheated oven for 20–25 minutes until golden Brush with the remaining honey, turn out onto a wire rack and leave to cool.

*5.* Cut into 12 slices and serve.

3

4

4

# CREAM PALMIERS

**MAKES:** *8* | **PREP:** *20 mins* | **COOK:** *15–18 mins*

**INGREDIENTS**

*40 g/1½ oz granulated sugar*
*225 g/8 oz puff pastry*
*400 ml/14 fl oz double cream, whipped*
*1 tbsp icing sugar, sifted*
*few drops vanilla extract*
*2 tbsp strawberry jam*

*1.* Preheat the oven to 220°C/425°F/Gas Mark 7. Dust a surface with half the granulated sugar and roll out the pastry to a 25 x 30-cm/10 x 12-inch rectangle.

*2.* Sprinkle the remaining granulated sugar over the pastry and gently roll over it with the rolling pin. Roll the two short sides of the pastry into the centre until they meet, moisten the edges that meet with a little water and press together gently. Cut across the roll into 16 even-sized slices.

*3.* Place the slices, cut side down, on a dampened baking tray. Use a rolling pin to flatten each one slightly.

*4.* Bake in the preheated oven for 15–18 minutes until crisp and golden brown, turning the palmiers over halfway through cooking so that both sides caramelize. Transfer to a wire rack and leave to cool.

*5.* Whip the cream with the icing sugar and vanilla extract until it holds soft peaks. Sandwich the palmiers together with the jam and whipped cream and serve within 2–3 hours of filling.

# CHOCOLATE FILO PARCELS

**MAKES:** *18* | **PREP:** *20–25 mins* | **COOK:** *10 mins*

**INGREDIENTS**

*85 g/3 oz ground hazelnuts*
*1 tbsp fresh mint*
*125 ml/4 fl oz soured cream*
*2 eating apples, peeled and grated*
*55 g/2 oz plain chocolate, melted*
*9 sheets filo pastry, about 15 cm/6 inches square*
*55–85 g/2–3 oz butter, melted, plus extra for greasing*
*icing sugar, for dusting*

*1.* Preheat the oven to 190°C/375°F/Gas Mark 5. Grease a baking sheet. Mix the nuts, mint and soured cream together in a bowl. Add the apples, stir in the chocolate and mix well.

*2.* Cut each pastry sheet into four squares. Brush one square with butter, then place a second square on top and brush with butter.

*3.* Place a tablespoon of the chocolate mixture in the centre, bring up the corners and twist together. Repeat until all of the pastry and filling have been used.

*4.* Place the parcels on the prepared baking sheet and bake in the preheated oven for about 10 minutes until crisp and golden. Remove from the oven and leave to cool slightly.

*5.* Dust with icing sugar and serve.

# VEGAN BLUEBERRY STRUDEL

**SERVES:** *4–6* | **PREP:** *15–20 mins* | **COOK:** *20–25 mins*

**NGREDIENTS**

*'00 g/7 oz blueberries*
*tbsp cornflour*
*00 g/3½ oz caster sugar*
*lain flour, for dusting*
*'70 g/9½ oz vegan filo pastry*
*0 g/1¾ oz vegan margarine, melted and cooled*
*cing sugar, for dusting*

*1.* Preheat the oven to 190°C/375°F/Gas Mark 5. Line a baking sheet with baking paper.

*2.* In a medium-sized bowl, mix the blueberries, cornflour and sugar together.

*3.* Place two sheets of pastry on a floured board, overlapping them slightly. Brush them with margarine and cover with two more sheets. of pastry. Brush these with margarine and top with a further two sheets of pastry.

*4.* Place the fruit mixture in a line close to one long edge of the pastry. Starting at that edge, carefully roll up the pastry, folding in the ends as you roll.

*5.* Transfer the strudel to the prepared baking sheet, brush the surface with the remaining margarine and bake in the preheated oven for 20 minutes, or until golden. Dust with icing sugar before serving warm or cold.

# TOFFEE CHOCOLATE PUFF TARTS

**MAKES:** *12* | **PREP:** *30 mins, plus chilling and cooling* | **COOK:** *25–30 mins*

**INGREDIENTS**

*375 g/13 oz ready-rolled puff pastry*
*140 g/5 oz plain chocolate, broken into pieces*
*300 ml/10 fl oz double cream*
*50 g/1¾ oz caster sugar*
*4 egg yolks*
*4 tbsp ready-made toffee sauce*
*100 ml/3½ fl oz whipping cream*
*cocoa powder, for dusting*

*1.* Line the base of a 12-hole muffin tin with rounds of baking paper. Cut out twelve 5-cm/2-inch rounds from the edge of the pastry and cut the remaining pastry into 12 strips. Roll out the strips to half their thickness and use a strip to line the sides of each hole. Place a round of pastry in each hole and press together to seal, making a tar case. Prick the bases and chill in the refrigerator for 30 minutes.

*2.* Meanwhile, preheat the oven to 200°C/400°F/Gas Mark 6. Put the chocolate into a heatproof bowl set over a saucepan of gently simmering water and heat until melted. Leave to cool slightly, then stir in the double cream.

*3.* Put the sugar and egg yolks into a bowl and beat together, then mix well with the melted chocolate. Place a teaspoon of the toffee sauce in each tart case, then divide the chocolate mixture between the tarts.

*4.* Bake in the preheated oven for 20–25 minutes, turning the tin around halfway through cooking, until just set. Leave to cool in the tin, then remove carefully. Whip the whipping cream until it holds soft peaks. Place a blob on top of each tart, dust with cocoa powder and serve.

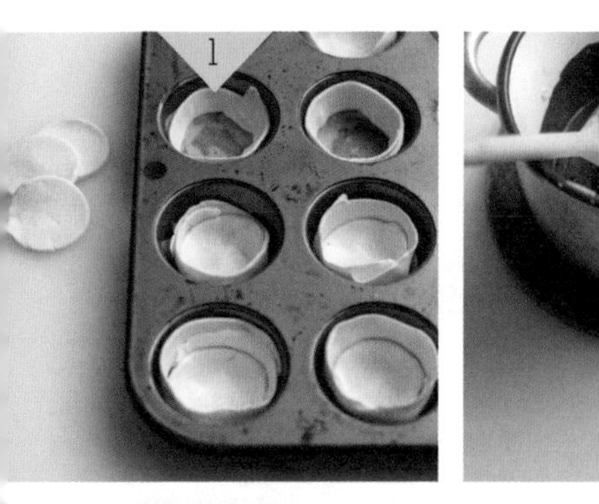
1

2

3

# STRAWBERRY ÉCLAIRS

**MAKES:** *16–18* | **PREP:** *20 mins* | **COOK:** *20–25 mins*

**INGREDIENTS**

**PASTRY**

*55 g/2 oz unsalted butter, plus extra for greasing*
*150 ml/5 fl oz water*
*8 tbsp plain flour, sifted*
*2 eggs, beaten*

**FILLING**

*200 g/7 oz strawberries*
*2 tbsp icing sugar*
*140 g/5 oz mascarpone cheese*

*1.* Preheat the oven to 220°C/425°F/Gas Mark 7. Grease 2 baking sheets. Heat the butter and water in a saucepan until boiling.

*2.* Remove from the heat, quickly tip in the flour and beat until smooth. Transfer to a bowl. Gradually beat in the eggs with a hand-held electric mixer, until glossy.

*3.* Spoon into a piping bag with a large plain nozzle and pipe up to eighteen 9-cm/3½-inch fingers onto the prepared baking sheets.

*4.* Bake in the preheated oven for 12–15 minutes, until golden brown. Cut a slit down the side of each éclair to release steam. Bake for a further 2 minutes, then transfer to a wire rack and leave to cool.

*5.* Hull the strawberries, then purée half of them with the icing sugar.

*6.* Finely chop the remaining strawberries and stir into the mascarpone cheese, then pipe or spoon the mascarpone mixture into the éclairs.

*7.* Serve the éclairs with the strawberry purée spooned over.

2
5
6

1
3
5

# FRESH CROISSANTS

**MAKES:** *6* | **PREP:** *30 mins* | **COOK:** *15–20 mins*

**NGREDIENTS**

*00 g/1 lb 2 oz strong white flour, sifted, plus extra for dusting*
*0 g/1½ oz caster sugar*
*tsp salt*
*tsp easy-blend dried yeast*
*00 ml/10 fl oz water*
*00 g/10½ oz cold butter, plus extra for greasing*
*egg, beaten with 1 tbsp milk, for glazing*

*1.* Preheat the oven to 200°C/400°F/ Gas Mark 6. Mix the dry ingredients in a large bowl, make a well in the centre and add the water. Mix to a soft dough, adding more water if too dry. Knead on a lightly floured surface for 5–10 minutes, or until smooth and elastic. Place in a large greased bowl, cover and leave in a warm place until doubled in volume.

*2.* Meanwhile, place the butter between two sheets of baking paper and flatten with a rolling pin to make a 5-mm/¼-inch thick rectangle. Transfer to the refrigerator until required.

*3.* Knead the dough for 1 minute. Remove the butter from the refrigerator. Roll out the dough on a well-floured work surface to a 46 x 15-cm/18 x 6-inch rectangle. Place the butter in the centre of the dough, folding up the sides and gently squeeze the edges together. With the short end of the dough towards you, fold the top third down and the bottom third up.

*4.* Give the dough a quarter turn, roll out to a rectangle as large as the original and fold again. If the butter feels soft, wrap the dough in clingfilm and chill. Repeat the rolling process twice more.

*5.* Cut the dough in half and roll out each piece into a 5-mm/¼-inch thick rectangle. Use a cardboard triangular template, base 18 cm/7 inches and sides 20 cm/8 inches, to cut out the croissants. Brush the triangles with the glaze. Roll into croissant shapes, tucking the point underneath. Brush again with the glaze. Place on a baking sheet and leave to double in volume. Bake in the preheated oven for 15–20 minutes until golden brown, then serve with a sweet or savoury filling.

CHAPTER FIVE

# BREAD & SAVOURY

# FIVE-GRAIN LOAF

**MAKES:** *1 loaf* | **PREP:** *20 mins, plus rising* | **COOK:** *25–30 mins*

**INGREDIENTS**

*300 g/10½ oz strong wholemeal flour, plus extra for dusting*
*225 g/8 oz strong white flour*
*1 tsp salt*
*100 g/3½ oz five-seed mix (including sesame, pumpkin, sunflower, hemp and linseeds)*
*7 g/¼ oz easy-blend dried yeast*
*1 tbsp soft light brown sugar*
*2 tbsp sunflower oil, plus extra for oiling*
*300 ml/10 fl oz lukewarm water*

*1.* Lightly oil a baking sheet. Mix the wholemeal flour, white flour, salt, seed mix and yeast in a large bowl. Stir in the sugar. Mix the oil and water together. Make a well in the centre of the dry ingredients and pour in the liquid. Mix with a knife to a soft sticky dough.

*2.* Turn out the dough onto a lightly floured surface and knead for 5–7 minutes, or until smooth and elastic. Shape the dough into a round ball and place on the prepared baking sheet. Dust the top of the loaf with wholemeal flour and leave in a warm place for 1–1½ hours, or until doubled in volume.

*3.* Meanwhile, preheat the oven to 220°C/425°F/Gas Mark 7. Bake in the preheated oven for 5 minutes. Reduce the oven temperature to 200°C/400°F/Gas Mark 6 and bake for a further 20–25 minutes, or until golden brown and the base sounds hollow when tapped with your knuckles. Transfer to a wire rack and leave to cool.

1
2
4

# SOURDOUGH BREAD

**MAKES:** *2 loaves* | **PREP:** *30 mins, plus standing & rising* | **COOK:** *30 mins*

**GREDIENTS**

*50 g/1 lb wholemeal flour*
*tsp salt*
*50 ml/12 fl oz lukewarm water*
*tbsp black treacle*
*tbsp vegetable oil, plus extra for brushing*
*ain flour, for dusting*

**TARTER**

*5 g/3 oz wholemeal flour*
*5 g/3 oz strong white flour*
*5 g/2 oz caster sugar*
*50 ml/9 fl oz milk*

*1.* To make the starter, put the wholemeal flour, white flour, sugar and milk into a non-metallic bowl and beat well with a fork. Cover with a damp tea towel and leave to stand at room temperature for 4–5 days, until the mixture is frothy and smells sour.

*2.* Sift together the flour and half the salt into a bowl and add the water, treacle, oil and starter. Mix well with a wooden spoon until a dough begins to form, then knead with your hands until it leaves the side of the bowl. Turn out onto a lightly floured surface and knead for 10 minutes until smooth and elastic.

*3.* Brush a bowl with oil. Shape the dough into a ball, put it into the bowl and put the bowl into a polythene bag or cover with a damp tea towel. Leave to rise in a warm place for 2 hours until the dough has doubled in volume.

*4.* Dust two baking sheets with flour. Mix the remaining salt with 4 tablespoons of water in a bowl. Turn out the dough onto a lightly floured work surface and knock back with your fist, then knead for a further 10 minutes. Halve the dough, shape each piece into an oval and place the loaves on the prepared baking sheets. Brush with the saltwater glaze and leave to stand in a warm place, brushing frequently with the glaze, for 30 minutes.

*5.* Preheat the oven to 220°C/425°F/Gas Mark 7. Brush the loaves with the remaining glaze and bake for 30 minutes until the crust is golden brown and the loaves sound hollow when tapped on the base with your knuckles. If they need further baking, reduce the oven temperature to 190°C/375°F/Gas Mark 5. Transfer the loaves to wire racks and leave to cool.

# SEEDED RYE BREAD

**MAKES:** *1 loaf* | **PREP:** *25 mins, plus rising* | **COOK:** *30–35 mins*

**INGREDIENTS**

*250 g/9 oz rye flour, plus extra for dusting*
*250 g/9 oz strong white flour*
*1½ tsp salt*
*1 tbsp caraway seeds*
*7 g/¼ oz easy-blend dried yeast*
*25 g/1 oz butter, melted*
*2 tbsp honey, warmed*
*300 ml/10 fl oz lukewarm water*
*sunflower oil, for oiling*

*1.* Mix the rye flour, white flour, salt, caraway seeds and yeast together in a large bowl and make a well in the centre. Mix the butter, honey and water together and pour into the well. Mix with a knife to a soft, sticky dough. Lightly oil a baking sheet.

*2.* Turn out the dough onto a floured surface and knead for 10 minutes, or until smooth and elastic. Shape into an oval and place on the prepared baking sheet. Slash the top of the loaf in a diamond pattern, lightly dust with flour and leave in a warm place for 1–1½ hours, or until doubled in volume.

*3.* Meanwhile, preheat the oven to 190°C/375°F/Gas Mark 5. Bake in the preheated oven for 30–35 minutes, or until the crust is a rich brown colour and the base of the loaf sounds hollow when tapped with your knuckles. Transfer to a wire rack and leave to cool.

# CRUSTY WHITE LOAF

**MAKES:** *1 loaf* | **PREP:** *30 mins, plus rising* | **COOK:** *30 mins*

**IGREDIENTS**

*egg*
*egg yolk*
*50–200 ml/5–7 fl oz lukewarm water*
*00 g/1 lb 2 oz strong white flour, plus extra for dusting*
*½ tsp salt*
*tsp sugar*
*tsp easy-blend dried yeast*
*5 g/1 oz butter, diced*
*nflower oil, for oiling*

*1.* Put the egg and egg yolk into a jug and lightly beat to mix. Add enough lukewarm water to make up to 300 ml/10 fl oz. Stir well.

*2.* Put the flour, salt, sugar and yeast into a large bowl. Add the butter and rub it in with your fingertips until the mixture resembles breadcrumbs. Make a well in the centre, add the egg mixture and work to a smooth dough.

*3.* Turn out onto a lightly floured surface and knead well for about 10 minutes, or until smooth. Brush a bowl with oil. Shape the dough into a ball, place it in the bowl and cover with a damp tea towel. Leave to rise in a warm place for 1 hour, or until the dough has doubled in volume.

*4.* Preheat the oven to 220°C/425°F/Gas Mark 7. Oil a 900-g/2-lb loaf tin. Turn out the dough onto a lightly floured surface and knead for 1 minute, or until smooth. Shape the dough into an oblong the length of the tin and three times the width. Fold the dough in three lengthways and place it in the tin with the join underneath. Cover and leave in a warm place for 30 minutes, or until it has risen above the tin.

*5.* Bake in the preheated oven for 30 minutes, or until firm and golden brown and the base of the loaf sounds hollow when tapped with your knuckles. Transfer to a wire rack and leave to cool.

# GLUTEN-FREE RED ONION, THYME & OLIVE FOCACCIA BREAD

**SERVES:** *9* | **PREP:** *20 mins, plus rising* | **COOK:** *30–35 mins*

**INGREDIENTS**

*450 g/1 lb gluten-free, wheat-free strong white flour*
*2 tsp dried yeast*
*2 tsp caster sugar*
*350 ml/12 fl oz lukewarm milk*
*2 eggs, beaten*
*butter, for greasing*
*1 garlic clove, finely chopped*
*10–12 black olives, stoned and halved*
*1 tbsp freshly grated Parmesan cheese, for sprinkling*
*rock salt and cracked black pepper (optional)*

**CARAMELISED ONION**

*50 g/1¾ oz butter*
*2 small red onions, thinly sliced*
*4–5 fresh thyme sprigs*

*1.* To make the caramelised onion, melt the butter in a small frying pan, add the onion and thyme and fry until the onion is soft and caramelized. Remove from the heat and leave to cool until needed.

*2.* Sift the flour into a bowl. In a separate bowl or jug, mix the yeast, sugar and milk and leave to stand at room temperature for 5–10 minutes until frothy. Mix in the eggs and add the liquid mixture to the flour and mix well.

*3.* Grease a 25 x 35-cm/10 x 14-inch baking tray and line with baking paper. Transfer the dough to the prepared tray, pushing it out to the edges. Cover with a clean damp tea towel and leave for about 45 minutes until it has doubled in size. Meanwhile, preheat the oven to 180°C/350°F/Gas Mark 4.

*4.* Spread the caramelised onion over the top of the bread, sprinkle with the garlic, olives and cheese, and salt and pepper to taste, if using. Press the toppings lightly into the bread using your fingers.

*5.* Bake in the preheated oven for 30–35 minutes until golden and crusty. Remove from the oven and leave to cool on a wire rack. The bread can be served hot or cold.

1
2
1 PINT
4

1
3
6

# PLAITED POPPY SEED BREAD

**MAKES:** *1 loaf* | **PREP:** *25 mins, plus rising* | **COOK:** *30–35 mins*

**INGREDIENTS**

*225 g/8 oz strong white flour, plus extra for dusting*
*1 tsp salt*
*2 tbsp skimmed milk powder*
*1½ tbsp caster sugar*
*1 tsp easy-blend dried yeast*
*175 g/6 oz water*
*2 tbsp vegetable oil, plus extra for oiling*
*5 tbsp poppy seeds*

**TOPPING**

*1 egg yolk*
*1 tbsp milk*
*1 tbsp caster sugar*
*2 tbsp poppy seeds*

*1.* Sift together the flour and salt into a bowl and stir in the milk powder, sugar and yeast. Make a well in the centre, pour in the water and oil and stir until the dough begins to come together. Add the poppy seeds and knead until fully combined and the dough leaves the side of the bowl. Turn out onto a lightly floured surface and knead well for about 10 minutes until smooth and elastic.

*2.* Brush a bowl with oil. Shape the dough into a ball, put it in the bowl, cover and leave to rise in a warm place for 1 hour, or until doubled in volume.

*3.* Oil a baking sheet. Turn out the dough onto a lightly floured surface, knock back and knead for 1–2 minutes. Divide into three equal pieces and shape each into a rope 25–30 cm/10–12 inches long.

*4.* Place the ropes side by side and press together at one end. Plait the dough, pinch the other end together and tuck underneath.

*5.* Put the loaf on the prepared baking sheet, cover and leave to rise in a warm place for 30 minutes. Meanwhile, preheat the oven to 200°C/400°F/Gas Mark 6.

*6.* To make the topping, beat the egg yolk with the milk and sugar. Brush the egg glaze over the top of the loaf and sprinkle with the poppy seeds. Bake in the preheated oven for 30–35 minutes, until golden brown. Transfer to a wire rack and leave to cool.

*7.* Serve plain or toasted as a lunchtime treat.

2
4
5

# WHITE BREAD ROLLS

**MAKES:** *24* | **PREP:** *20 mins, plus rising* | **COOK:** *20–25 mins*

**NGREDIENTS**

*eggs*
*tbsp vegetable oil*
*0 g/2¼ oz caster sugar*
*tbsp xanthan gum*
*5 g/3 oz potato flour*
*80 g/1 lb 1 oz white rice flour, plus extra for dusting*
*50 g/9 oz tapioca flour*
*5 g/3 oz buckwheat flour*
*tsp easy-blend dried yeast*
*tsp salt*
*00 ml/10 fl oz lukewarm milk*

*1.* Preheat the oven to 190°C/375°F/Gas Mark 5. Line two baking trays with baking paper.

*2.* Combine the eggs, oil and sugar in a large bowl and mix well using a food processor or hand-held electric mixer.

*3.* Add the xanthan gum, potato flour, white rice flour, tapioca flour, buckwheat flour, yeast and salt and mix well, gradually adding the milk until a thick dough forms.

*4.* Transfer the dough from the bowl to a floured surface and knead for 1–2 minutes. Divide the dough and shape it into 24 balls, using extra flour if necessary to prevent the dough sticking.

*5.* Place the rolls on the prepared trays, cover with a clean damp tea towel and leave to rise at room temperature for 45 minutes–1 hour until they have almost doubled in size.

*6.* Bake in the preheated oven for 20–25 minutes until golden brown. Remove from the oven and leave to cool on a wire rack.

# SAGE SHARE & TEAR BREAD

**SERVES:** *8* | **PREP:** *20 mins, plus rising* | **COOK:** *40 mins*

**INGREDIENTS**

*1 tsp salt*
*350 g/12 oz strong white bread flour*
*1½ tsp easy-blend dried yeast*
*200 ml/7 fl oz lukewarm water*
*3 tbsp olive oil, plus extra for oiling*
*1 red onion, finely sliced*
*8–10 fresh sage leaves, finely chopped*

*1.* Place the salt in a mixing bowl and sift in the flour. Add the yeast and make a small well. In a separate bowl mix the water and 1 tablespoon of the oil together. Pour into the dry ingredients and mix to a dough.

*2.* Turn out the dough onto a lightly oiled surface and knead for about 10 minutes, or until the dough has a smooth, elastic texture. Alternatively, use a dough hook in a food processor and knead on a low setting for 5 minutes.

*3.* Transfer the dough to a lightly oiled bowl, cover and set aside to rise in a warm place for about 1 hour, or until the dough has doubled in size.

*4.* Meanwhile, heat the remaining oil in a large saucepan over a low heat. Add the onion and cook for 8–10 minutes, or until soft. Stir in the sage and remove from the heat. Knead the onion and sage mixture into the dough until evenly distributed, and the dough has returned to its original volume. Divide the dough into eight equal-sized pieces and roll each piece into a ball.

*5.* Grease a 20-cm/8-inch cake tin. Place the bread balls into the prepared tin, cover and set aside to rise in a warm place for about 30 minutes. Meanwhile, preheat the oven to 200°C/400°F/Gas Mark 6.

*6.* Bake in the preheated oven for 20–25 minutes, until golden. Transfer to a wire rack and leave to cool.

1

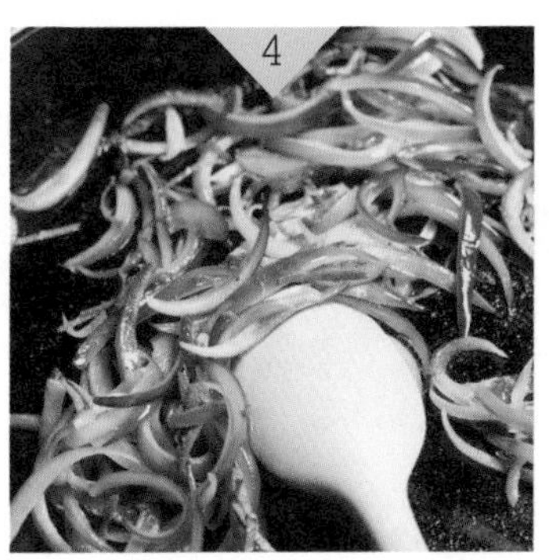
4

4

1
4
5

# VEGAN & GLUTEN-FREE CHICKPEA BREAD

**SERVES:** *12* | **PREP:** *15 mins, plus standing* | **COOK:** *35–40 mins*

**IGREDIENTS**

*50 g/9 oz gram flour*

*00 ml/1½ pints water*

*tbsp extra virgin olive oil*

*alt and pepper (optional)*

*esh rosemary sprigs, to garnish*

*1.* Put the flour into a large mixing bowl. Gradually whisk in the water using a balloon whisk or a hand-held electric mixer. Whisk until completely smooth, then add salt and pepper to taste, if using. Set the bowl aside for 3 hours to allow the batter to thicken.

*2.* Preheat the oven to 180°C/350°F/Gas Mark 4.

*3.* Put the oil into a 33 x 23-cm/13 x 9-inch baking tray with a rim of at least 1 cm/½ inch.

*4.* Give the batter a quick stir with a wooden spoon and pour it into the prepared tray. Arrange the rosemary in a decorative pattern on top of the batter.

*5.* Carefully put the tray into the preheated oven – the oil underneath the wet batter tends to make it slide about in the tray. Bake for 35–40 minutes, or until golden brown and firm. Leave to cool for 5 minutes in the tray before slicing.

# WHOLEMEAL CARROT ROLLS

**MAKES:** *8* | **PREP:** *20 mins, plus resting & rising* | **COOK:** *12–15 mins*

**INGREDIENTS**

*250 g/9 oz strong white flour plus extra for dusting*
*250 g/9 oz strong wholemeal flour plus extra for sprinkling*
*1 sachet easy-blend dried yeast*
*1½ tsp salt*
*300 ml/10 fl oz lukewarm water*
*2 tbsp olive oil*
*175 g/6 oz carrots, finely grated*
*vegetable oil, for oiling*

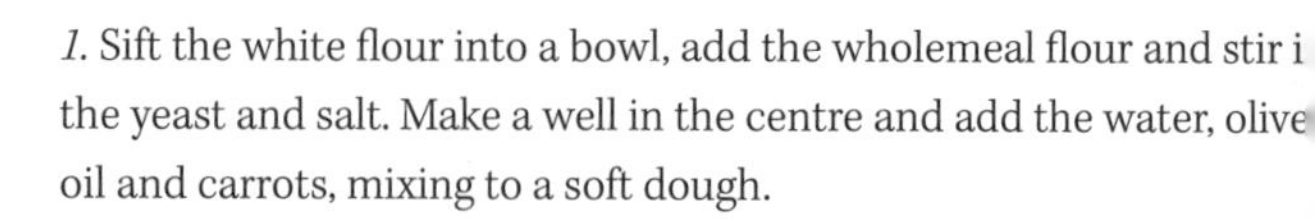

*1.* Sift the white flour into a bowl, add the wholemeal flour and stir i the yeast and salt. Make a well in the centre and add the water, olive oil and carrots, mixing to a soft dough.

*2.* Turn out the dough onto a lightly floured surface and knead for about 10 minutes until smooth. Place the dough in a bowl, cover an leave to rest for 5 minutes.

*3.* Brush a baking sheet with vegetable oil. Turn out the dough onto a lightly floured surface and lightly knead again until smooth. Divid into eight pieces, shape each piece into a ball and arrange on the prepared baking sheet, well spaced to allow room for spreading.

*4.* Cover and leave in a warm place for about 1 hour, or until double in volume. Meanwhile, preheat the oven to 220°C/425°F/Gas Mark 7

*5.* Sprinkle the rolls with a little wholemeal flour and bake in the preheated oven for 12–15 minutes, or until golden brown. Transfer t a wire rack and leave to cool.

# GLUTEN-FREE PARMESAN & GARLIC ROLLS

**MAKES:** *12* | **PREP:** *25 mins, plus rising* | **COOK:** *15–20 mins*

**IGREDIENTS**

*tbsp olive oil, plus extra for oiling*
*garlic cloves, crushed*
*)0 g/14 oz gluten-free, wheat-free strong white flour plus extra for dusting*
*½ tsp salt*
*sachet gluten-free easy-blend dried yeast*
*5 g/2 oz finely grated Parmesan cheese*
*)0 ml/10 fl oz lukewarm water*
*ilk, for glazing*

*1.* Oil a baking sheet. Heat the oil in a saucepan, add the garlic and gently stir-fry for about 1 minute without browning. Remove from the heat and leave to cool slightly.

*2.* Sift together the flour and salt into a bowl, then stir in the yeast and three quarters of the cheese. Make a well in the centre and add the water and garlic oil, stirring to a soft dough.

*3.* Turn out the dough onto a lightly floured surface and lightly knead until smooth. Divide into 12 pieces and shape each piece into a smooth round.

*4.* Place the rounds on the prepared baking sheet and cut a deep cross into the top of each one with a sharp knife. Cover and leave in a warm place for about 1 hour, or until doubled in volume. Meanwhile, preheat the oven to 200°C/400°F/Gas Mark 6.

*5.* Brush the tops of the rolls with milk and sprinkle with the remaining cheese. Bake in the preheated oven for 12–15 minutes, or until firm and golden brown. Transfer to a wire rack and leave to cool.

1
1
2

# WALNUT & PECORINO SCONES

**MAKES:** *10* | **PREP:** *20 mins* | **COOK:** *15 mins*

**NGREDIENTS**

*50 g/1 lb self-raising flour plus extra for dusting*
*inch of salt*
*5 g/3 oz butter, diced plus extra for greasing*
*0 g/1¾ oz caster sugar*
*0 g/1¾ oz pecorino cheese, grated*
*00 g/3½ oz walnut pieces*
*00 ml/10 fl oz milk*

*1.* Preheat the oven to 200°C/400°F/Gas Mark 6. Grease a baking sheet. Sift the flour and salt into a large bowl. Add the butter and rub it in with your fingertips until the mixture resembles fine breadcrumbs. Stir in the sugar, cheese and walnuts. Add enough of the milk to bring the mixture together in a soft but not sticky dough.

*2.* Gently roll out the dough on a lightly floured work surface to a thickness of 2.5–3 cm/1–1¼ inches. Use a 6-cm/2½-inch round biscuit cutter to stamp out rounds (make the scones smaller or larger if you prefer).

*3.* Put the rounds on the prepared baking sheet and bake in the preheated oven for 15 minutes, or until golden and firm. Remove from the oven and leave to cool on a wire rack.

# PAIN AU CHOCOLAT CINNAMON ROLLS

**MAKES:** *12* | **PREP:** *20 mins, plus cooling & standing* | **COOK:** *25–30 mins*

**INGREDIENTS**

*100 g/3½ oz plain chocolate, broken into pieces*
*320 g/11 oz ready-rolled puff pastry*
*25 g/1 oz unsalted butter, melted*
*2 tbsp caster sugar*
*1½ tsp ground cinnamon*

*1.* Put the chocolate into a heatproof bowl set over a saucepan of gently simmering water and heat until melted. Remove from the heat, stir until smooth, then leave to cool for 15 minutes, stirring occasionally.

*2.* Unroll the pastry and place on a board. Generously brush with some of the butter. Leave to stand for 10 minutes, then spread the cooled chocolate all over the buttered pastry. Mix the sugar and cinnamon together in a bowl, then sprinkle over the chocolate.

*3.* Roll up the pastry, Swiss roll-style, from one long side, then brush all over with more of the butter. Chill in the refrigerator for 15 minutes. Preheat the oven to 220°C/425°F/Gas Mark 7. Use the remaining butter to grease a 12-hole cupcake tin.

*4.* Using a serrated knife, slice the pastry roll into 12 even-sized rounds. Place each round, cut-side up, in a hole in the prepared tin.

*5.* Bake in the preheated oven for 15–20 minutes, or until risen and golden brown. Leave to cool in the tin for 5 minutes, then transfer to a wire rack. Serve warm or cold.

1

2
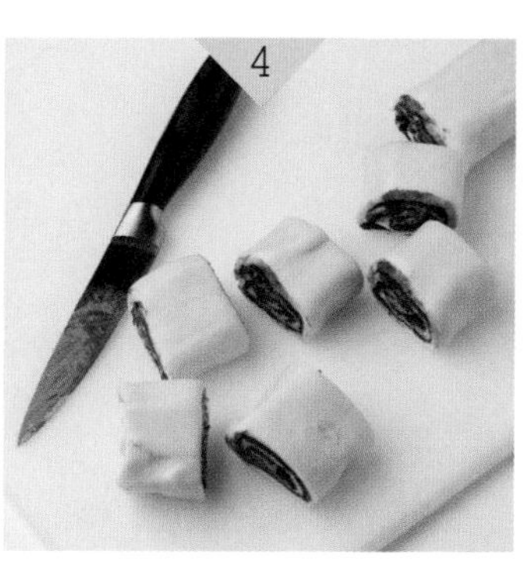
4

# CHOCOLATE & SAFFRON BRIOCHES

**MAKES:** *12* | **PREP:** *20 mins, plus rising* | **COOK:** *12–15 mins*

**INGREDIENTS**

*¼ tsp saffron strands*
*3 tbsp boiling water*
*55 g/2 oz butter, melted*
*250 g/9 oz strong white flour*
*pinch of salt*
*1 tbsp caster sugar*
*1 x 6 g/⅛ oz sachet easy-blend dried yeast*
*2 eggs, beaten*
*25 g/1 oz plain chocolate, broken into squares*
*milk, for glazing*
*vegetable oil, for oiling*

*1.* Add the saffron to the water and leave to cool completely.

*2.* Lightly brush 12 individual brioche tins or a 12-hole fluted bun tin with some of the butter.

*3.* Sift together the flour, salt and sugar into a bowl and stir in the yeast. Add the saffron, saffron liquid, eggs and remaining butter and mix to a soft dough.

*4.* Knead until smooth, then cover and leave in a warm place for 1–1½ hours, or until doubled in volume.

*5.* Knead briefly, then shape three quarters of the dough into 12 even sized balls. Place a ball in each of the prepared tins and press a piece of chocolate firmly into each ball. Shape the remaining dough into 12 small balls with pointed ends. Brush with milk and press one ball into each bun, sealing well.

*6.* Cover with oiled clingfilm and leave in a warm place for 1½ hours or until doubled in volume.

*7.* Preheat the oven to 200°C/400°F/Gas Mark 6. Brush the brioches with milk and bake in the preheated oven for 12–15 minutes until firm and golden.

*8.* Turn out the brioches and serve warm.

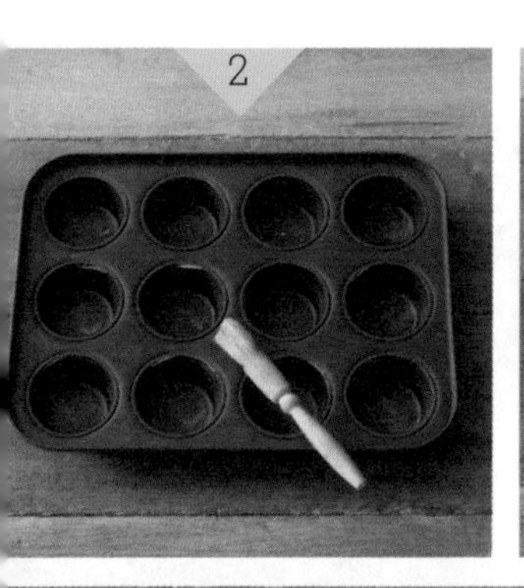
2

3

5

# WHOLEWHEAT SPINACH, PEA & FETA TART

**SERVES:** *6* | **PREP:** *30 mins, plus chilling & cooling* | **COOK:** *1 hour–1 hour 10 mins*

**INGREDIENTS**

*15 g/½ oz unsalted butter*
*3 spring onions, thinly sliced*
*200 g/7 oz baby spinach*
*100 g/3½ oz fresh shelled peas*
*3 eggs*
*250 ml/9 fl oz milk*
*100 g/3½ oz feta cheese, drained and finely crumbled*
*115 g/4 oz cherry tomatoes*
*sea salt and pepper (optional)*

**PASTRY**

*115 g/4 oz unsalted butter, cut into cubes*
*225 g/8 oz wholemeal plain flour, plus extra for dusting*
*2 eggs, beaten*
*salt and pepper (optional)*

*1.* To make the pastry, put the butter and flour in a mixing bowl and season with salt and pepper, if using. Rub the butter into the flour until it resembles fine crumbs. Gradually mix in enough egg to make a soft but not sticky dough. Turn out the dough onto a lightly floured surface and gently knead, then roll it out to a round a little larger than a 25-cm/10-inch loose-based flan tin. Lift the pastry over the rolling pin, ease it into the tin and press it into the sides. Trim the pastry to stand a little above the top of the tin to allow for shrinkage, then prick the base with a fork. Cover with clingfilm and chill in the refrigerator for 15–30 minutes. Meanwhile, preheat the oven to 190°C/375°F/Gas Mark 5.

*2.* To make the filling, melt the butter in a frying pan over a medium heat. Add the spring onions and cook for 2–3 minutes, or until soft. Add the spinach, turn the heat to high, and cook, stirring, until wilted. Set aside to cool. Cook the peas in a small saucepan of boiling water for 2 minutes. Drain, then plunge into iced water and drain again. Crack the eggs into a jug, add the milk, season to taste with salt and pepper, if using, and beat with a fork.

*3.* Line the pastry case with a large sheet of baking paper, fill with baking beans and bake in the preheated oven for 10 minutes. Remove the paper and beans and bake for a further 5 minutes.

*4.* Drain any cooking juices from the spring onions and spinach into the eggs. Put the onion mixture in the pastry case, add the peas, then sprinkle over the cheese. Pour in the egg mixture and dot the tomatoes over the top. Bake for 40–50 minutes, or until set and golden. Leave to cool for 20 minutes, then serve.

# CHEESE, CHILLI & POTATO EMPANADAS

**MAKES:** *12* | **PREP:** *25–30 mins, plus chilling & standing* | **COOK:** *23–30 mins*

**NGREDIENTS**

**ASTRY**

*25 g/15 oz plain flour*
*4 tsp salt*
*75 g/6 oz chilled unsalted butter, diced*
*egg*
*0 ml/2 fl oz water*

**ILLING**

*25 g/8 oz fleshy green chillies*
*50 g/5½ oz mozzarella cheese, shredded*
*15 g/4 oz feta cheese, crumbled*
*2 red onion, finely chopped*
*tsp dried oregano*
*tsp cumin seeds, crushed*
*4 tsp salt*
*4 tsp pepper*
*potato, cooked and diced, about 175 g/6 oz total weight*
*egg yolk*
*tbsp milk*

**AUCE**

*25 ml/8 fl oz soured cream*
*uice of ½ lime*
*–3 tbsp chillies in adobo sauce*
*tbsp chopped fresh coriander*

*1.* To make the pastry, mix the flour and salt together in a food processor. Add the butter, egg and water and pulse briefly until clumps form. Do not overwork the dough. Shape into a flattened ball and chill in the refrigerator for 30 minutes.

*2.* To make the filling, put the chillies on a baking sheet and grill under a very hot grill for 8–10 minutes, turning once, until the skin is black. Cover with a tea towel and set aside for 10 minutes. Peel off the skin, remove the stems and seeds and roughly chop the flesh. Preheat the oven to 220°C/425°F/Gas Mark 7. Line a baking sheet with a silicone sheet.

*3.* Put the chillies, mozzarella cheese, feta cheese, onion, oregano, cumin seeds, salt and pepper into a bowl and lightly mix with a fork.

*4.* Put the prepared baking sheet into the preheated oven. Divide the dough into 12 even-sized pieces and shape into balls. Flatten slightly, then roll out each ball to a 15-cm/6-inch round, neatening the edges with a cookie cutter.

*5.* Place 2 tablespoons of the cheese mixture and a few pieces of potato in one half of each round. Moisten the edges with water, fold over and seal. Crimp the edges with a fork. Mix the egg yolk and milk in a small bowl. Brush over the empanadas. Place on the preheated baking sheet and bake for 15–20 minutes until golden.

*6.* Meanwhile, mix the sauce ingredients together in a serving bowl. Serve the empanadas warm or at room temperature with the sauce.

# BROCCOLI, PANCETTA & BLUE CHEESE GALETTE

**SERVES:** *4* | **PREP:** *15 mins* | **COOK:** *30–35 mins*

**INGREDIENTS**

*1 sheet ready-rolled puff pastry (half a pack)*
*225 g/8 oz broccoli florets (halved if necessary)*
*125 g/4½ oz pancetta*
*1 small red onion, sliced*
*100 g/3½ oz Gorgonzola cheese or Roquefort cheese, chopped*
*pepper (optional)*
*toasted pine nuts, to garnish*

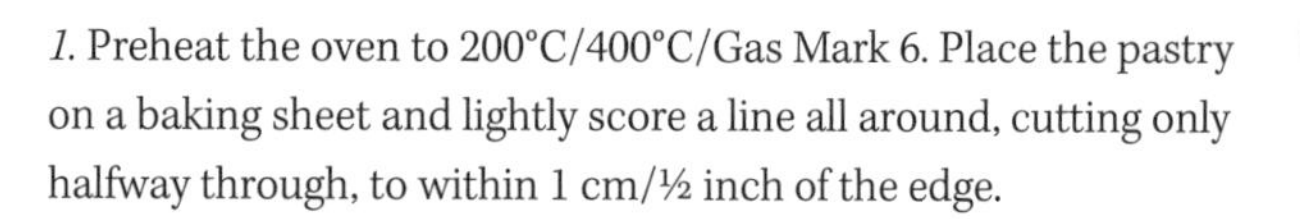

*1.* Preheat the oven to 200°C/400°C/Gas Mark 6. Place the pastry on a baking sheet and lightly score a line all around, cutting only halfway through, to within 1 cm/½ inch of the edge.

*2.* Put the broccoli in a steamer and steam for 4–5 minutes, until just tender. Drain.

*3.* Fry the pancetta with the onion, stirring, until golden. Stir in the broccoli and season to taste with pepper, if using.

*4.* Spread the filling over the pastry, leaving the border clear.

*5.* Scatter the pieces of cheese evenly over the top.

*6.* Bake in the preheated oven for 25–30 minutes, until the pastry is risen and golden.

*7.* Sprinkle with pine nuts and serve warm.

# VEGAN SWEET POTATO & PECAN FILO PARCELS

**MAKES:** *12* | **PREP:** *20–25 mins* | **COOK:** *10–12 mins*

**NGREDIENTS**

- *large sweet potato, baked, peeled and mashed, about 280 g/10 oz total weight*
- *0 g/2¼ oz shelled pecan nuts, finely chopped*
- *⅛ tsp freshly ground nutmeg*
- *½ tsp very finely chopped fresh ginger*
- *tsp coconut sugar*
- *tsp lemon juice*
- *x 44 x 24-cm/17½ x 9½-inch filo pastry sheets*
- *tbsp hazelnut or olive oil, for brushing*
- *cing sugar mixed with ground cinnamon, for dusting*

*1.* Preheat the oven to 200°C/400°F/Gas Mark 6. Line a baking tray with a silicone sheet.

*2.* Mix the sweet potato and half the nuts together in a bowl. Add the nutmeg, ginger, sugar and lemon juice, mixing well with a fork.

*3.* Unroll the sheets of filo pastry and stack on a board with the long edge facing you. Using a ruler or metal edge as a guide, slice crossways into three 44 x 8-cm/17½ x 3¼-inch strips. Work with one strip at a time, covering the remaining strips with a clean damp tea towel to prevent them drying out.

*4.* Lightly brush the upper surface of one filo strip with oil. Sprinkle with a few of the remaining nuts.

*5.* Place a tablespoon of the sweet potato mixture in the bottom left-hand corner of the pastry strip and lightly mould it into a rough triangle. Fold the pastry over diagonally to form a triangle. Continue to fold in triangles until you reach the end of the strip.

*6.* Brush both sides of the parcel with oil and place on the baking tray. Repeat with the remaining filo strips.

*7.* Bake in the preheated oven for 10–12 minutes, turning halfway through the cooking time, or until golden and crisp.

*8.* Transfer to a wire rack and leave to cool slightly. Lightly dust all over with the icing sugar and cinnamon mixture. Serve immediately.

# CHARD & RICOTTA FILO PIE

**SERVES:** *9* | **PREP:** *20 mins* | **COOK:** *50 mins–1 hour*

**INGREDIENTS**

*900 g/2 lb rainbow chard*
*55 g/2 oz butter, plus extra for greasing*
*2 leeks, sliced*
*2 garlic cloves, thinly sliced*
*3 tbsp mixed fresh herbs, such as thyme, marjoram and flat-leaf parsley*
*400 g/14 oz ricotta cheese*
*55 g/2 oz freshly grated Parmesan cheese*
*¼ tsp nutmeg*
*2 eggs, beaten*
*12 sheets filo pastry*
*olive oil, for brushing*
*55 g/2 oz pine nuts*
*sea salt and pepper (optional)*

*1.* Chop the chard stems into chunks. Slice the leaves into thin ribbons. Heat the butter in a large frying pan over a medium heat. Add the leeks and chard stalks, cover and fry for 5–7 minutes until soft. Add the chard leaves, garlic and herbs. Cover and gently fry until the leaves are tender. Tip the vegetables into a colander and drain.

*2.* Beat together the ricotta cheese, Parmesan cheese, nutmeg and eggs in a large bowl. Mix in the drained vegetables. Season to taste with salt and pepper, if using.

*3.* Preheat the oven to 190°C/375°F/Gas Mark 5. Grease a 23 x 30-cm/9 x 12-inch roasting tin. Place a sheet of filo pastry in the prepared tin, trimming to fit as necessary. Brush with oil and sprinkle with a few pine nuts. Add 5 more filo sheets, lightly brushing each one with oil and sprinkling with pine nuts.

*4.* Pour in the filling and level the surface. Cover with 5 more sheets of filo pastry, brushing each sheet with oil and sprinkling with pine nuts. Add the final sheet and brush with oil.

*5.* Using a sharp knife, cut through all the pastry and filling layers to make nine squares.

*6.* Bake in the preheated oven for 35–40 minutes, until golden and crisp. Cut into squares and serve hot or at room temperature.

2

3

4

2
2
3

# MINI CHICKEN POT PIES

**MAKES:** *12* | **PREP:** *30 mins* | **COOK:** *45 mins, plus cooling*

**NGREDIENTS**

*5 g/1 oz butter, plus extra for greasing*
*tbsp olive oil*
*00 g/1 lb 2 oz boneless, skinless chicken breasts, cut into 1-cm/ ½-inch cubes*
*leek, white and green parts separated and thinly sliced*
*tbsp plain flour, plus extra for dusting*
*50 ml/15 fl oz chicken stock*
*tbsp dry white wine*
*tbsp roughly chopped fresh tarragon*
*tbsp roughly chopped fresh parsley*
*tbsp chopped capers*
*50 g/1 lb 7 oz ready-made plain shortcrust pastry, chilled*
*egg yolk mixed with 1 tablespoon of water, for glazing*

*1.* Preheat the oven to 180°C/350°F/Gas Mark 4. Lightly grease a 12-hole muffin tin.

*2.* Heat the butter and oil in a frying pan over a medium heat. Add the chicken and white leek slices and fry, stirring, for 10 minutes, or until the chicken is golden brown and the leeks are soft. Sprinkle the flour over the top and mix together, then add the stock and wine. Simmer for 5 minutes, stirring occasionally, until the sauce has thickened and the chicken is tender and cooked through. Add the green leek slices and cook for 2 minutes, or until the leeks are just soft. Sprinkle over the tarragon, parsley and capers and leave to cool.

*3.* Thinly roll out two thirds of the pastry on a lightly floured surface. Using a plain 10-cm/4-inch round cutter, stamp out 12 rounds. Gently press the rounds into the prepared tin, re-rolling the trimmings as needed. Brush the top edges of the pie cases with a little of the egg glaze, then spoon in the filling.

*4.* Roll out the reserved pastry and any trimmings on a lightly floured surface. Using a plain 7-cm/2¾-inch round cutter, stamp out 12 rounds. Arrange these on top of the pies, pressing the edges together well to seal. Brush the pastry with egg glaze; add leaves cut out from rolled pastry trimmings using a sharp knife, then brush with the egg glaze.

*5.* Bake in the preheated oven for 25 minutes, or until golden brown. Leave to cool in the tin for 5 minutes, then transfer to serving plates. Serve hot or cold.

# INDEX

This edition published by Parragon Books Ltd in 2017
LOVE FOOD is an imprint of Parragon Books Ltd

Parragon Books Ltd
Chartist House
15–17 Trim Street
Bath BA1 1HA, UK
www.parragon.co.uk/love-food
www.parragon.com.au/love-food



ISBN 978-1-4748-6900-3

Printed in China

Introduction by Sarah Bush
Edited by Fiona Biggs
Cover photography by Al Richardson

The cover shot shows the Sweet Potato, Coconut & Lime Cupcakes on page 50

## *Notes for the Reader*

This book uses both metric and imperial measurements. Follow the same units of measurement throughout; do not mix metric and imperial. All spoon measurements are level: teaspoons are assumed to be 5 ml, and tablespoons are assumed to be 15 ml. Unless otherwise stated, milk is assumed to be full fat, eggs and individual fruits and vegetables are medium, pepper is freshly ground black pepper and salt is table salt. Unless otherwise stated, all root vegetables should be peeled prior to using.

The times given are an approximate guide only. Preparation times differ according to the techniques used by different people and the cooking times may also vary from those given.